TOTAL
CONFIDENCE

TOTAL CONFIDENCE

PHILIPPA DAVIES

PIATKUS

*For Sue Berry, who lived with confidence and
courage and gave these qualities to others*

First published in 1994 by
Judy Piatkus (Publishers) Ltd of
5 Windmill Street, London W1P 1HF

Reprinted 1994

First paperback edition 1995

Reprinted 1996

Reprinted 1997

Reprinted 1998

A catalogue record for this book is
available from the British Library

ISBN 0 7499 1347 9 hbk
ISBN 0 7499 1434 3 pbk

Edited by Maggie Daykin
Designed by Paul Saunders
Drawings by Min Cooper

Set in Monophoto Times by
Datix International Limited, Bungay, Suffolk
Printed and bound in Great Britain by
Bookcraft Ltd, Midsomer Norton, Avon

Contents

Introduction

W HEN I started to research in preparation for writing this book, I found that remarkably little had been written about the subject of confidence. And though I discovered several authorities who had produced good books on single, specific techniques of confidence-building, such as assertiveness or speaking skills, there was nothing that gave a comprehensive overview of approaches. Trying to link what I had read to my own experiences, it became clear that, above all, confidence was about dealing with uncertainty. And uncertainty could best be dealt with by looking at it from several angles. I resolved to do this in my book.

Facing Change with Confidence

We live in an age of uncertainty, one in which the world is changing faster and more dramatically than it has ever done before. In the last fifty years, there have been tremendous advances in technology and communication, and many of us have had to acquire new skills in order to retain our present work or, indeed, prepare ourselves for a new career. Clearly, in such circumstances, self-confidence is a vital asset. It helps us to face up to many other pressures, too.

Political and economic boundaries have shifted significantly, and sometimes whole communities have had to adjust to dramatically altered lifestyles. Even the traditional values of church and family have waned. A UK survey carried out for the *Sunday Times*, for example, showed that only 7 per cent of the population now live in a family with 2.4 children, where the father works and the mother stays at home. Research centres such as the Henley Centre for Forecasting, predict an even greater rise in the number of single adults of all ages, living alone. There are indications that this is by no means always out of necessity; increasing numbers now prefer to live alone for a variety of reasons. But *anyone* who lives alone essentially needs self-confidence.

In fact, whatever our individual circumstances are right now, we *all* need self-confidence in this age of uncertainty. Our ways of living and working *are* changing dramatically and while this can often be exciting, it is also unsettling. Viewed positively, all this change means that most of us have more choice in regard to how we work, where we holiday, what we eat, our healthcare and education, but it also means a greater number of decisions have to be made – by us. When our lives are not going as we want them to, should we change our jobs, our partners, our houses – or our attitudes? Now, more than ever, we need guidelines to help us live our lives effectively.

This book is all about guidelines. With guidelines, decision-making becomes much easier. *Total Confidence* will help you to identify guidelines you already use, and to develop new ones. It looks at how you can order your thoughts and experiences to build self-confidence. It also demonstrates how you can look and sound confident, and describes confidence techniques for specific situations such as making conversation with strangers, speaking effectively at meetings, or dealing with conflict and aggressive behaviour. Finally, it helps you to acquire more advanced confidence skills: techniques to get you noticed and to help others develop their confidence.

In short, *Total Confidence* aims to be comprehensive, helpful and entertaining. Confidence-building can and should be an enjoyable experience; one where you apply ideas and techniques and experiment with them to get the most out of life. I have learnt a great deal while researching this book and had great fun trying out the various techniques. I hope you will do the same. But before you do, you may find it useful – and encouraging – to read my story, briefly. Several times during the writing of this book, it occurred to me that that very task takes quite a bit of confidence – which is something *I* have not always had.

Growing Confidence

I was born in West Wales, where I lived until I went away to read drama at university in Hull. My family background was very ordinary: one grandfather played the violin in pubs for a living and the other was a railway engine driver. My parents both worked very hard to better themselves, and my father eventually became the only non-graduate government officer at his level in the country. Although he never had an opportunity to go to university, he encouraged us as children to make that our goal, and loved to stir us to heated debate on political and philosophical issues. At the same time, we were urged never to regard disagreement as personal.

Despite such a positive, outgoing example in my father, I was by nature shy – and like a lot of shy people I was attracted to acting. Spending time being other people seemed an easier prospect than having to deal with my rather insecure self. After university, I spent seven years pursuing an acting career, working on average about six months in every year. When I did get acting work, I kept being cast in seemingly endless productions of *Under Milk Wood*. This time of my life was enormously frustrating. I hated the regular rejection, which often seemed to be based on not looking and sounding right, and I was burning to be successful at something. A lot of the time I felt rejected and miserable, but I also learnt quite a lot about how people project confidence – by observing other hopefuls who attended the same auditions. I studied their manner of speech, dress, attitude and general self-presentation, and tried to assess who was most likely to get a particular part – what made the successful ones outstanding.

The highlight of these years was starting my own pop group, 'Les Bon-Bons', and although we had a short-lived career, we achieved the rare distinction of getting banned for being sexist. Our song, *Loretta's a Sweater Girl Now*, about a girl who bought a tight sweater which changed her life, offended some of the rather humourless people running the alternative cabaret venue where we performed.

It was a precarious lifestyle and eventually I decided it was time to try something new – but preferably still connected with acting or performance. In my late twenties, I was lucky enough to get a bursary to go to the Central School of Speech and Drama, to study to be a voice teacher. On this course I learnt a great deal about how people speak with confidence. And going back to being a student in my late twenties was a revelation in other ways, too. I realised that I had all sorts of resources that I wasn't using. For example, from the small actors' co-operative agency that I'd recently been involved in running, I had learnt all sorts of business skills. The course took a year and at the end of it, with two associates, I set up a training company: Voiceworks.

Less drama – more success

We were women with a mission – to take aspects of theatre and media training to people in business and the professions, so that they could improve their presentation and communication skills. After a shaky start, during which we subsidised the business by teaching in drama schools, we started to make some money. When I look back at that time, it makes me smile. We were naive, optimistic and completely overawed by the business world. We were also very nervous about speaking to potential customers on the phone and face-to-face, but we were determined to succeed. We irrepressibly banged on doors until they opened.

Years of relative failure in the acting business had done me a great service – it had toughened my attitude towards rejection. If people didn't want what I was selling, then I would just move on to someone else who did. Because I had no idea of what to expect in running a small business, and few assumptions (but some fantasies) about how the business world worked, I was open to all sorts of opportunities and possibilities. It was at this time that I was invited to collaborate on a book, and soon found myself with an agent and a publishing contract.

That was eight years ago, and since then Voiceworks has grown. From the outset we have run courses that are as much about confidence as they are about communication. In my view, the two subjects are inextricably linked. We began by running evening workshops, open to the general public, on dealing with the fear of public speaking. Our first venue was the YMCA, in a room directly below an aerobics class. It was hardly ideal – but very useful when it came to talking about voice projection.

Further study – and collaboration

So where does my expertise in the psychology of confidence come from? Well, once Voiceworks was up and running, I was able to pursue an increasing interest in this subject. I read widely and studied lots of different approaches to self-development, from psychoanalysis to

Native American fire ceremonies. I also wrote another two books, and became involved in writing and presenting television and radio programmes connected with my interest. This, in turn, led to me training people such as television newsreaders in how to refine their skills.

I'm now making my interest in psychology official by doing postgraduate work in the Organisational Psychology department of London University.

It is my belief and experience that confidence grows when we view life as a process of continuing education. Daunting challenges, such as addressing medical conferences – which I now do regularly – represent milestones in my own confidence journey. I was petrified when I addressed my first group of doctors, but experience and experiment in what they want to hear has increased my confidence. No doubt further challenges – new opportunities for personal growth – lie ahead.

But this is just *my* viewpoint. Working in collaboration with other trainers and psychologists, I have heard just as plausible arguments for other priorities and milestones being important in building confidence. On our confidence-building courses, several experts with different viewpoints and ideas about exactly what generates confidence work together. The content of this book, then, is based on other people's views and experiences as well as my own, on stories from people who have been on our courses, interviews, and academic research.

Part One

Thinking
WITH
Confidence

1 *Defining Confidence*

'YOU are never dedicated to something you have complete confidence in. No one is fanatically shouting that the sun is going to rise tomorrow. When people are fanatically dedicated to political or religious faiths or any other kind of dogmas or goals, it's always because these dogmas or goals are in doubt' (Robert T. Pirsig: *Zen and the Art of Motorcycle Maintenance*).

Has a would-be helpful relative, friend or colleague ever told you: 'What you need is more confidence.'? If someone has, then you'll know how frustrating the vagueness of the advice can be. How can you get more of something when you are not quite sure what it is? And if, as Robert T. Pirsig says, complete confidence doesn't go with fanatical dedication, dogmas and goals, how easy is it to know what direction to follow in order to build it up?

The word 'confidence' comes from the Latin, *confidere*, meaning to trust – as in: 'I have every confidence in your ability.' Confidence is also about trusting ourselves to make the most of our lives, to have resources to deal with the unexpected, and to engage constructively with others. In this book, we shall especially be looking at how we trust ourselves to carry out these activities at work, but the techniques described will also prove of enormous benefit in many other aspects of your life.

In aiming to define confidence, we find that it has many meanings. We speak of 'sharing confidences', meaning exchanging private thoughts with others. We hear of people being the victims of 'confidence tricks', describing behaviour that abuses their trust. We even describe people as 'having too much confidence', meaning they have too high an opinion of themselves, beyond their capabilities. Someone like the late Robert Maxwell, for instance, was both a confidence trickster and had too much confidence in the success of his schemes.

Now, advertisers would have us believe that confidence can be *bought*. As a visitor to this planet, it would be easy to think from television advertising, and newspaper and magazine advertising and editorial, that confidence comes from a wide range of sources: diets, breath fresheners, the latest fashions, a new hairstyle, or even tampons or toothpaste. Unfortunately, acquiring and inspiring confidence is not that quick or that simple.

Valuable Commodity

What we can be sure about, is that confidence is an extremely valuable commodity. With confidence, we can feel comfortable in standing up and speaking off the cuff to a group of strangers. We can be as happy in company as we can be in solitude. We can feel like a winner and a success in life rather than a downtrodden victim. With confidence, we can know ourselves and select wisely how and in what ways we want to develop. We can enjoy life-changes (both predictable and unpredictable), as well as secure routine. We can express our sense of humour and fun, without worrying about social correctness or causing unwitting offence to others.

With confidence, we can help our children to be confident, too, so that they enjoy a great advantage in life. We can put other people at their ease, and help the less confident to become more so. We can perform better in all sorts of situations: exams, interviews, meetings, arguments, even in bed. Quite simply, with confidence we live our lives better.

Now this is not just my opinion. As well as common sense telling us that confidence is of great value, the theory of academic psychology is full of references to 'self-efficacy', meaning how confident we feel about our effectiveness; and 'expectation', meaning how confident we feel about the likelihood of success. Our levels of self-efficacy and expectation will influence how motivated we are and how well we perform. They will affect how we view changing jobs, and accepting difficult challenges. In addition to our performance at work, our general levels of motivation are also affected by these qualities.

But perhaps confidence is most valuable because it makes us happy. With confidence, we cope better with any knocks that life brings. Realistically, we can see the upside of events, as well as the downside. When we look at a glass containing wine, we see it as half-full rather than half-empty. We define confidence as being much more about 'I can' than 'I can't'.

Three Perspectives

Confidence-building has to be worked at, and it can be achieved, whatever your present confidence level may be. This book is wide-reaching in its subject matter and treatment of approaches, because as individuals we vary so much in our needs for confidence. Some of us may feel it, but not project it. So we know exactly the direction we would like to take – for instance, in a project at work – but we have trouble communicating our purpose to others. Or we may feel quite wobbly inside – for instance when we're attending a job interview or appraisal – but be quite successful at concealing our anxiety. Even so, we would like to feel better and have more constructive messages inside our heads.

And because we are complex as individuals, confidence-building is demanding. We need to get to know ourselves: what blocks we have about confidence, and whether we are overlooking areas that others may think important. We need to understand how we are thinking, and to appreciate that sometimes we are unrealistically harsh on ourselves. We need to appreciate how to send out behaviour signals that can be interpreted by others as showing confidence, as there is not much point in feeling confident inside if the rest of the world fails to read you as such.

We need to realise too, that confidence-building is not just about ourselves. Were we able to build confidence purely through our own positive thinking, then there would be no need to write this book. As it happens, though, our relationships with other people matter greatly, as does the situation. We can find ourselves having our confidence under-mined only when we are in the company of specific individuals who behave in a certain way. Or we may realise that it is just in particular situations – meeting strangers for instance, or having to disagree with people – that we find our confidence falling.

My aim in *Total Confidence* is to look at the subject from these three

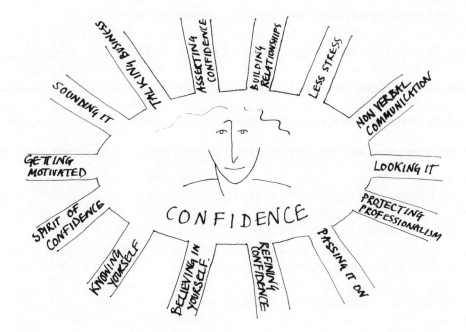

perspectives: what it means to you, to other people and in the context of the situation. This is a book as much for those who want to understand and help others better, as it is for those who want to develop themselves.

*T*otal Confidence Map

Fortunately, our individual needs are catered for by there being many different and effective approaches to confidence building. In exploring different directions, each of us can discover our own most appropriate route or routes. We can see confidence as being the highly-desirable centre of a map, with lots of routes leading to it. Each chapter of this book covers one of what I consider to be the most clear and accessible routes, there are fourteen in all, as shown in the diagram above.

You will find it helpful to identify from this map which routes are most relevant to you. But, first of all, identify the resources you already have, by answering the following questions, then checking your score against my analysis.

	Yes	No
1. Do you know your strengths and weaknesses?	☐	☐
2. Do you have clear beliefs which support you in life?	☐	☐
3. Do you enjoy how you look?	☐	☐
4. Do you enjoy talking to strangers?	☐	☐
5. Are you able to encourage others to feel more confident?	☐	☐
6. Are you motivated much of the time?	☐	☐
7. Can you control your stress levels?	☐	☐
8. Do you command respect at work?	☐	☐
9. Are you comfortable in turning people down?	☐	☐
10. Would you say that most of the time you have a high level of self-esteem?	☐	☐
11. Do you like the sound of your own voice?	☐	☐
12. Are you good at influencing others?	☐	☐
13. Do you know how you judge others?	☐	☐
14. Do you use body language effectively?	☐	☐
15. Do you create a good impression on others most of the time?	☐	☐

Now score one point for each of your 'yesses'. A total of three or more for questions 1, 2, 6, 10 and 13 suggests that you are already thinking with confidence. What about questions 4, 7, 9, 11 and 12? Thee or more again, then congratulations; you are already speaking with confidence. Now your 'yes' answers for questions 3, 5, 8, 14 and 15. Three or more and you are well on your way to projecting confidence. Your scores indicate which parts of this book are most and least relevant to you.

Now let's take a closer look at which areas you need to develop:

         Yes No

1. Do you sometimes feel shy and self conscious? ☐ ☐

2. Would you like to help others to grow in confidence? ☐ ☐

3. Do you sometimes look ill at ease? ☐ ☐

4. Would you find it difficult to describe your personality? ☐ ☐

5. Are you uncomfortable in dealing with conflict? ☐ ☐

6. Are you uncertain about how to dress to look your best? ☐ ☐

7. Do you avoid thinking about spiritual matters and the 'meaning of life'? ☐ ☐

8. Do you avoid speaking to groups? ☐ ☐

9. Do you sometimes appear unprofessional? ☐ ☐

10. Do you hold lots of negative beliefs about yourself? ☐ ☐

11. Do you feel often that you lack purpose? ☐ ☐

12. Would you like a higher profile at work? ☐ ☐

13. Do you feel pulled in many directions? ☐ ☐

14. Are you hyper-sensitive to criticism? ☐ ☐

15. Do you often feel stressed out? ☐ ☐

Once more, count your 'yes' answers. Three or more to questions 4, 7, 10, 11 and 13 indicates that you will find Part One of this book: 'Thinking with Confidence' especially useful. If you scored three or more on questions 1, 5, 8, 14 and 15, then you will find Part Two: 'Speaking with Confidence' most useful. Scoring three or more on questions 2, 3, 6, 9 and 12 indicates that Part Three: 'Projecting Confidence' will be most beneficial to you.

Part One: Thinking with confidence   is about how our psychology influences our confidence levels. It deals with how we think and feel, how we play roles, different personality types, and motivation. It also looks at ways of developing a confident spirit.

Part Two: Speaking with confidence   is about how confidence affects the way we communicate. We look at how we talk with confidence, assertiveness, building relationships, how to influence others, deal with conflict and control the effects of stress.

Part Three: Projecting confidence   deals with using confidence to make an impact on others, to convey professionalism and how we can spread confidence so that we inspire and encourage others.

This division reflects three important areas of confidence that concern the many people who have attended the confidence-building courses which my company provides.

If it has never occurred to you that you need confidence in a particular area, then it is unlikely that you do. Congratulate yourself on that strength and focus on building confidence in the area or areas where you have decided there is scope for growth, for another definition of confidence must be that it is a secure knowledge of our own resources.

Confronting Confidence

On courses, we ask people to consider the following important questions about their attitudes towards confidence. How would you answer? See how your responses compare with the ones given below.

Q. *Are we born confident?*

A. Most parents with babies and young children say that we are. To date, a genetic influence on shyness and lack of confidence has not been identified, but it is possible that in the future one could be discovered. Recent studies by university researchers in the USA have suggested that genes play a role in sexual preferences and, possibly, alcoholism. For the present we can assume that babies are burbling bundles of confidence, expecting attention whenever they cry to be cuddled, fed or have their nappy changed.

Q. *How do we lose it?*

A. It can be very helpful to identify when and how we think we lost confidence, because that may well give us clues as to why we react as we do in the present. Consider Thomas's experience, for example.

Thomas, who came on a course, had everyone wondering why he was there. He is the chief executive of a thriving company, has great social skills and is charming and well-presented. All the other participants found him a great talker *and* a great listener. But he was almost phobic about speaking in public. This had determined his management style: he favoured 'management by walking about', chatting to people on the shop floor rather than formally addressing his employees en masse. As we got to know him better, he told us that when he was a schoolboy he had made a speech at a school event and it went – according to his perceptions – disastrously. Anxious to do well, he had spoken from fairly detailed notes which, unfortunately, were not on numbered sheets. In his nervousness, he dropped them and took several minutes to put them back in order. His perfectionist father had been present and had made Thomas feel ashamed and humiliated afterwards, calling him a fumbling young fool in front of his schoolmates. After hearing this tale, we could all understand why Thomas felt as he did about public speaking.

We lose confidence, then, via bad experiences, through lack of positive encouragement and praise, through being made to feel that we are bad or inadequate in some way. Often it is members of our families – parents, sisters and brothers – who cause us to have these experiences. Messages such as: 'Oh, her brother's the bright one', or 'He's an awkward little devil', or 'You're so selfish', deflate our confidence. Authority figures such as teachers and bosses, too, can knock our confidence, especially when we receive strong messages from them at an impressionable age. We're told: 'You must try harder', 'Stop talking', or 'You can't be in the choir, you're tone deaf.'

As well as losing confidence via such personal experiences and messages from people who are close to us, the type of society we live in can also affect our confidence. Living in a society, for instance, which generally fails to consider the disabled, doesn't help the disabled to feel confident. When people are attacked or disadvantaged on the grounds of their race or sex, their confidence is being unfairly knocked. Despite an increasingly mobile society, class is still a particularly strong influence in this country – especially if you want to make it to the top in the city or a venerable institution. Different sectors of our society are continually putting out messages about whose face fits where.

Q. *Are there any pay-offs in not being confident?*

A. This may seem like an odd consideration, but it is a crucial one in building confidence. We can't hope to become more confident unless we know what pay-offs or benefits there have been for *not* being confident in the past and what *new* pay-offs we will get once we are more confident.

When we lack confidence, we tend to avoid challenges and therefore we don't risk failing at these challenges. We may even 'look good' to others because they don't see, hear or know about our failures. The discount side is: no risk, no progress. When we lack confidence, we also often have an appeal for people who consider themselves to be strong, rescuing types. They will look after us and protect us, and while we are dependent on them for this protection, they are dependent on us to confirm their self image. There is an exchange going on that usually suits both parties, for a short time at least. We often see this exchange between the shy child and an overly-protective parent. Though the pay-offs for becoming more confident can seem very obvious, it is worth thinking as specifically as possible about what they will be for you, particularly in the light of the following question and answer.

Q. *Are there any* **disadvantages** *in being confident?*

A. This is a question many people feel most uncomfortable answering, because it is much easier to think that everything that confidence brings is good. And if people weren't sometimes envious and self-centred but always valued confidence and felt very confident themselves, then you might be right to think that increasing your confidence can only bring benefits.

Realistically though, increasing your confidence can have its downside. Some people will envy you; they will see you demonstrating a quality they would dearly love to have themselves. And because of this envy, they may gossip about you vindictively, describe you as ruthless and single-minded, even plot to sabotage you and influence others against you. Your new persona will threaten them and they will try to undermine you. Take, for example, the husband who – when his wife is returning to work on her first day – comments, 'You're not going dressed like that are you?'

Another repercussion of increasing confidence, can be that other people actively or passively withdraw their support. If you're regarded as 'someone who can look after themselves', 'a success', 'a well-rounded individual', or, as the magazines would describe it, 'a woman or man who juggles their life effectively', then other people may keep their distance and not offer you support. Indeed, they might find the idea that you ever need support clashes with their rose-tinted image of you. More subtly, perhaps, if you're obviously getting more confident, then you may find that the friend who used to call you once a week only calls you once a month, although as far as you can see there have been no changes in *her* circumstances to cause her to do that.

So, after all, is it worth building confidence? Of course; we owe it to ourselves to live our lives to the full, rather than as mere shadows of what we might be. And besides helping us to live fulfilling lives, confidence can be highly contagious. It can inspire others and help them to achieve, too. It may have an unsettling effect on some relationships for a while, but with mutual regard the worthwhile ones will survive – and grow.

Total Confidence is written in the belief that people can keep changing, learning and growing throughout their lives. Though change can be challenging, if we can see the rewards are worth it, then we will succeed. Throughout the following chapters there are practical exercises and techniques which you can use to build confidence. I've called these Confidence Tricks. The first one, below, helps you identify these important rewards:

CONFIDENCE TRICK: Reaping rewards

Choose a situation that is important to you, one in which you would like to think, speak or project yourself with greater confidence. It could be meeting new clients, standing up to a difficult boss, or going for a tough interview. What is the effect of what you are doing in that situation at the moment? And what will be the rewards for you from being much more confident in the future? You may find it helpful to write these rewards down so that they stick in your mind as positive goals to aim for.

Now that we've examined the diverse meanings of confidence and begun to think of the benefits it can bring, let's take the second of our routes to confidence . . . believing in yourself.

2 *Believing in Yourself*

CONFIDENCE KEY: Self esteem, failure and fear, self-talk and healthy thinking

---

JANE is a manager in a finance company, and recently she was encouraged by her boss to apply for a much higher position. Though she wouldn't have considered going for the job herself, she agreed with her boss that her experience and achievements matched what they were looking for perfectly. After some nervous deliberation, she did apply. The interview, however, was an ordeal – as she later described:

'All the way there and throughout the interview, I could hear a nagging little voice in my head saying things like, "Who do you think you are?" and "You've really over-reached yourself this time." This voice kept putting me down, and during the interview it really affected my performance. I couldn't see myself as having a right to be there. I felt ill at ease and as though I was an impostor. In consequence, I appeared apologetic and nervous to the panel, and I didn't even get short-listed. Since then, I've given myself a project of building my self-esteem and I'm managing to keep that nagging little critic under control. The next time an opportunity for promotion comes along, I intend to be the successful applicant.'

A Question of Standards

In this chapter, we look at the core of confidence: self esteem and what we believe about ourselves. We look at the fears that block our confidence, and how we can use healthy thinking-messages that will support, rather than sabotage our endeavours. You will find this chapter especially useful if you sometimes suffer from 'not good enough-itis' and, as Jane did, give yourself negative messages which only serve to make you feel bad. You will find it useful too, if you tend to be very hard on yourself and undermine your confidence in that way. Perhaps you are always setting yourself unrealistically high standards, or wanting to please everyone, or taking responsibility for everyone's problems, so that sometimes you feel completely drained.

There are two important themes in this chapter. The first is that we become more confident when our ideas about ourselves, other people and events closely match reality. So if you believe yourself to be of little value, yet are surrounded by evidence to the contrary – family, friends and colleagues who obviously appreciate your worth – then it's worth taking stock of this evidence. What often happens, though, is that our negative self-talk is powerful and practised, to the extent that we project it on to other people. Ignoring what is really going on, we assume that everyone present is thinking the same as we are. Richard, a young solicitor, is a perfect example. He is very conscientious and able, but also highly self-critical, as his account makes plain:

'My boss was taken sick last month, and I had to take over running the Property Department. We deal with quite large properties and some very wealthy clients. But my first meeting with clients in my new capacity was a complete nightmare. I kept thinking: "You're bungling this", "You're appearing completely inadequate", and "They think you're a complete idiot". I was taken by surprise when one of the partners later called me to say that the clients were most impressed with my knowledge and authority, especially in one so young! I had imagined they were judging me in the same way that I was judging myself.'

The second important theme of this chapter is that of tolerance. Healthy thinking is about appreciating your own individuality and that of other people. It's about allowing yourself to be who you want to be, rather than conforming to some ideal your parents, husband or managing director has set up for you. We need to cherish just how uniquely individual we all are, while valuing, too, how much we can achieve by expressing what we have in common with one another, and working together towards collective goals.

Cultural Values and Pressures

In this country, we have strong cultural values about modesty and self-effacement. It is 'not done' to draw attention to oneself, to make a great show of wanting to succeed and enjoying the limelight. This is in marked contrast to American culture. To varying degrees, cultural values get passed down to us from a very early age, via our families. If you were brought up in a family where you were encouraged to 'be seen and not heard', or to 'keep quiet until you have something worth saying', then this will inevitably affect your ability to project confidence. That is not to say, however, that you cannot overcome such a start in life.

Our families also often convey to us a sense of where they are in society. For instance, if your family held a strong sense of: 'We know our place and it's not very high up the ladder', then this may lower your self-esteem. On the other hand, if you were fortunate enough to be brought up in a family which held a sense of: 'We're well-placed and advantaged in society', then this feeling of privilege may boost your sense of self-worth.

If we were not brought up to have high self-esteem then we are going to have to work hard to develop it. *But when the cause of a problem has been in the past, we may unwittingly sustain its effect in the present.* We may constantly behave in ways that continually reactivate the problem: 'They told me I was bad, so that's what I'll damn well be!' And though the problem is from the past, the solution must be found in the present. Constantly reminding ourselves, for instance, about a deprived childhood, is not constructive. Understanding the negative effects of a deprived childhood and deciding to change these effects in the present, is. Though we may need professional help from a therapist or counsellor to do this, depending on the degree of deprivation and its effects.

As we grow up, too, many of us get used to negative criticism. Our parents, remember, didn't receive lessons in bringing up children. They may have labelled us as 'bad', 'stupid' or 'lazy' when, very often, what they meant was that *our behaviour* warranted these descriptions. As children, we look to our parents to tell us who we are, and to give us our identity. On the receiving end of these messages, we interpret them as permanent judgements. Whereas our parents will have been describing *our behaviour*, we interpret their messages to be about *our identity*. The effect of these negative messages is that we become highly self-critical. We dwell on our failures and inadequacies and forget our successes and strengths.

Several months ago, Kate came up to me at the end of a conference at which I had been a speaker. Looking slightly embarrassed, she told me that she had attended a conference a couple of years ago, where I had also spoken. She said that her life had been what she described as a 'shambles' at that point. She had just got divorced, had been made redundant and was completely without direction. Quite a lot of this she had felt was to do with her unhappy childhood: her parents had drink and money problems, and were sometimes violent towards her. Her self-esteem had been very low. The purpose of this earlier conference had been to motivate and inspire women to change their lives, and it seemed that with Kate we had succeeded. She said it had made her realise she could go out and make something of her life. She had been on several courses, had joined a support group and explored all sorts of avenues of self-improvement. She now had a good job and a pleasant flat she loved. And she felt that her life was still improving.

All this was related with slight self-consciousness. Kate was not someone who enjoyed talking about herself, but she had a very clear purpose in coming to talk to me. She wanted to show me evidence that we can change our lives. As it happened, I had noticed her in the audience when I was speaking; she was distinctive because of her attractive and stylish appearance. I was quite moved by her story.

CONFIDENCE TRICK: Building Self-Esteem

- We can build our self-esteem by keeping a valuable 'bank' of achievements we are proud of, and examining what we've got on reserve, when our confidence is low. Often, when we're feeling low, we overlook resources we've used effectively on other occasions.

- Confront limiting messages and definitions you were given by your family in the past. What were you told or how were you reacted to, that made you feel inadequate? Do these messages need to apply in the present? Or are you now just using the definitions as a habitual way of thinking about yourself? Think about what you've done that contradicts these negative messages from your family. No modesty is allowed here – give yourself due credit, and don't move on from this page until you've filled these in:

My greatest achievement is _____

My second greatest achievement is _____

My third greatest achievement is _____

• Abandon modesty even further and fill in the following:

I'm absolutely brilliant at _____

I'm very good at _____

I'm quite good at _____

• Read through all of your answers several times and commit them to memory. The next time your self-esteem feels wobbly, remind yourself of these statements, or look back at this page and read them through again. You will feel bolstered by them.

Facing Failure

'Try again. Fail again. Try harder. Fail better.' SAMUEL BECKETT

All of us have experienced shame and humiliation at some point or another in our lives, usually when we've failed at something. These experiences can leave us extremely sensitive to failure, so that we avoid it whenever possible. We don't take risks or accept challenges. When we do fail, as all human beings do sometimes – and the more successful the person the higher their incidence of failure is likely to have been – then we may avoid taking any personal responsibility for it.

This is a pity, because we are denying ourselves the opportunity to learn from our failures so we have a better chance of success next time. Think of an incident in the past six months where you wished you had been more confident. What caused the problem? The situation? Other people? You? Or a combination of influences? Most crucially, which of these influences is it easiest for you to change? The answer, of course, is yourself – whether it be a change of attitude or reaction. When we take reasonable responsibility for events, then we give ourselves power to do something about them. For example, a row at work may not have been your fault, but if you had spoken up, then you would not have been treated as a doormat by your boss.

But, of course, we can't be responsible for everything. Most of us are small cogs in big wheels and influences such as luck, our genes, politics and economics will play their part in how easy it is for us to succeed or fail. I like my partner's definition of luck as being 'the intersection of preparation and opportunity'. Blaming failure entirely on luck or genes is too defeatist. There are fine examples of people who have overcome such influences and gone on to achieve great things. Stephen Hawking, the eminent physicist and best-selling author, has motor neurone disease. Oprah Winfrey, the chat show host and media mogul, was abused and deprived as a child and has a persistent weight problem. Emma Nicholson, prominent Conservative MP and campaigner has hearing difficulties. David Blunkett, shadow cabinet member at the time of writing and Labour MP, is blind.

Rather than focusing on their disadvantages and carrying them around as heavy psychological baggage, throughout their lives, these individuals have all focused on their strengths and abilities, and developed them. Undoubtedly they have all been persistent and courageous. They will all have failed many times, but they will have learnt from these failures. And there are many other people with less evident or publicised disadvantages, who also prefer to live their lives as seekers of opportunities wherever they can use their particular strengths, rather than as victims of ill-fortune.

I can't emphasise too strongly that if you feel confused and traumatised by your past then you should seek professional help. However, if you are carrying around 'psychological baggage' that is not so serious, you may simply want to dump it in the following ritual exorcism.

CONFIDENCE TRICK: Dumping off Baggage

- It can be very useful to enact 'dumping off' bad experiences physically. It's almost as though the symbolic ritual helps us move on from the past, to a brighter rite of passage in the future.

- Pinpoint an instance when you have felt extremely uncomfortable about failing. Write it down on a piece of paper or draw it.

- Now, tear the paper up into tiny pieces and throw it away. Or, if the ritual element really appeals to you, either flush it down the toilet or burn it, for added drama.

Credit and Criticism

Our resistance to accepting and learning from failure can be very strong. We may have developed habitual responses which prevent us facing up to what's really happening. The threat of having to admit to inadequacy is too much for us and our fragile self-esteem, so we develop untested and often dubious theories about what causes certain effects. For example, we may try to preserve our self-esteem by taking the credit for good results ourselves, while blaming bad results on the situation. Perhaps you've noticed at your place of work or study, that when people are praised they will often say: 'It's because I planned well', or 'I felt very enthusiastic' – taking the credit for their achievements *themselves.* When negative criticism is given, however, they will often say, 'There wasn't enough time to plan', or 'the subject's not interesting', blaming the *situation* for their failure.

Another bias we have is towards blaming *other people's personalities.* Let's say your company is merging with another, and the merger is not going smoothly. You will probably hear a lot of sentiments along the lines of, 'Well, it's the chief executive's personality causing this.' Whereas in reality, the situation will be contributing to what's going on, as well. Perhaps there is an important difference in senior level contracts that need to be rationalised, or a need to make compatible two different computer systems – or perhaps there is an unforeseen negative reaction from key suppliers.

Perhaps in your office you've got a woman or man who plays the 'fall-guy' for much that goes wrong. Their unfortunate personality will be blamed for everything. Of course, in reality when your team fails to agree over a project deadline and the fall-guy's being blamed, a whole lot of other factors will play a part. For instance, who gave the fall-guy the job? Why hasn't his or her manager dealt with this negativity? Why do the rest of you respond too sensitively to the fall-guy's bad attitude and allow him or her to intimidate you?

And it's not just in office politics that we like to blame individual personalities unrealistically. In national and international politics too, we are always trying to find hanging dogs for whatever has gone wrong. How neat and satisfactory and conclusive to say that the UK recession was *all* the fault of Margaret Thatcher, or Nigel Lawson, or Norman Lamont. Whereas again, in truth, several factors in the situation might have contributed: the boom and bust nature of economics, a worldwide recession, and the collapse of business confidence. Individual personalities may well have contributed to the recession; but no single individual will have caused it.

You may even attribute your own lack of self-esteem to one personality – that of your mother. Some approaches to psychology actually encourage people to blame their mother for all their misfortunes. Now, of course, mothers – and fathers – are important in our personality development. But your mother's personality developed, too. She was influenced by her parents, her siblings, the type of society and life experience *she* encountered as she grew up. Her early conditioning, and environment will have determined to a large extent how she later treated you. Things are very rarely *all* 'mummy's fault'.

Negating Responsibility, Losing Power

Let's examine one more instance of how we record events in terms of our own behaviour being determined by the *situation* and other people's behaviour being determined by their *personalities*. Simon has had a bad job interview and is now rationalising this to himself and his naturally sympathetic girlfriend:

'Well, I was very nervous, because it was the first interview I'd had for months. And the panel members were not exactly helpful. In fact, they were brusque and impersonal. The woman was aggressive and the two men were just, well, impatient and disinterested. One of them started looking at his watch almost before the first question was fired at me.'

So, in Simon's interpretation, his behaviour could be excused by the *situation* – while that of the panel was down to their *unfortunate dispositions*. According to Simon, the situation determined his behaviour, implying that there was nothing he could do about his nervousness. The panel members, on the other hand, were just a thoroughly bad lot. Simon makes no allowance for situational factors such as the day being hot, the room badly ventilated, and his position as last and not particularly well-prepared candidate. Convenient leaps of logic such as these are very common.

In order to increase our confidence, we need to be realistic and logical about what causes us to lack confidence. When Simon blames the panel and takes no responsibility himself, he is implying that for things to improve other people have to change. This takes power away from Simon – presumably he will have to wait until he gets a decent interview panel before he gets a job. Whereas if he takes some personal responsibility for improving matters, and decides to hone his interviewing skills, he will make himself more powerful. He will be able to perform to his own satisfaction at interview, whatever the panel is like. He may even be able to make an indifferent panel sit up and take notice.

And remember, it is much easier to take responsibility for changing our own attitudes and behaviour, than it is to attempt to change other people's.

My final point about failure rests with some phenomenal success stories from the world of books:

- James Joyce's *Dubliners* was rejected by twenty-two publishers.

- Richard Bach's *Jonathan Livingston Seagull* was rejected by eighteen publishers. It went on to sell seven million copies in the USA alone.

- Twenty-one publishers turned down *M.A.S.H.* by Richard Hooker before it was finally accepted and became a massive bestseller.

So persistence pays . . .

Fear and Confidence Blocks

It is not just a fear of failure that prevents us from gaining in confidence. Having heard many stories from many people about confidence blocks, it seems to me that almost any confidence crisis is about one or more of the following four fears:

- Fear of isolation and rejection.

- Fear of loss of identity and distinctiveness.

- Fear of loss of control.

- Fear of lack of competence.

Let us take a closer look at each one of these.

Fear of isolation and rejection

Robert is an outgoing man in his late twenties, who works in a large retail organisation. He enjoys his role of managing people and dealing with customers and their needs. His confidence plummets when he has to stand up for what he believes in at meetings. He hates conflict and disagreement. And he's aware that this makes him a poor manager, in some ways. He doesn't always stand up for his team, when he should.

Like many of us, Robert enjoys feeling like a team-player engaged in productive collaboration. What he is overlooking though is that healthy debate and disagreement – not necessarily related to personal rejection – can be the most effective means of reaching solutions that everyone feels involved in. If you fear debate, you will not enjoy negotiation or being made to stand up for what you want and what you believe in. You may therefore find yourself being bullied by others and going along with things that you don't really agree with. You may take decisions that make you popular, rather than which are wise. If you are very concerned about isolation, then this will make it difficult, if not impossible, for you to get to the top, as it is often lonely there.

This fear of confrontation or isolation can also affect our confidence when faced with the prospect of moving, changing jobs, even taking promotion. In our personal lives, it may mean we stay in a rotten relationship, rather than face up to life alone. We can help ourselves to overcome this fear through working on the rogue rules we may be using (see next section), and we can work on these rules constructively to deal with all the fears described in this section.

Fear of loss of identity

Do you know people who are always awkward, who will argue for the sake of it, who don't appear to listen to others or to hear alternative points of view? If we feel at all shaky about who we are, then we may employ any or all of these tactics to impose our identity on other people. We may have become adept at getting in first in meetings, holding forth at length when really we don't have much to say, undermining our more conciliatory colleagues by challenging them in an aggressive fashion.

This is a fear that expresses itself through an 'It's you or me, sunshine' attitude. In fact – boxing and wrestling matches aside – situations and relationships are rarely that black and white. The trouble with this fear is that if we are so anxious to establish our own identity and afraid of being swamped and overpowered by others, then we will miss a great deal of what is going on around us. And in the long term this will be to our detriment. Not least, we may find that colleagues begin to display the same scant regard for our opinions and ideas that we have shown to them.

This fear can prevent people getting involved in relationships with others. So, intimacy, teamwork and managing people successfully becomes very difficult. They may end up being lonely, because other people will want to avoid their bullying tactics.

The problem can be overcome by learning about the psychology of relationships and acquiring practical relationship building skills – such as becoming a good listener and genuinely considering what the other person says, rather than rushing in with your own agenda. Some form of team or group activity in your leisure time may also help you to feel more 'connected', such as a sport or outdoor activity where you *have* to trust others.

Fear of loss of control

Lynne is a hospital doctor in her mid-forties who has had a successful career and also raised a family. Her job has changed so that she now has to do a lot more influencing of, and committee work with, managers. Lynne's profession and the hectic lifestyle she's chosen have made her supremely effective at taking control. The demands of her committee work though seem to be undermining her confidence. She complains of having to deal with the unexpected – having to talk to medical staff, the board of management or the media – at short notice. When pressed, it's not just these new demands that are getting to her. Her three teenage children have become wildly rebellious and for the first time in her life, she feels important facets of her life are out of control.

The fear of losing control is a very common one, and we may cope with it by being excessively ordered and trying to prepare for every eventuality. We have to learn to accept that we cannot prepare for *everything* that might happen, and that sometimes we need just to go with the flow. We need to sit back and absorb what is happening and *then* establish guidelines and structure for how to deal with it. This fear can also prevent us having fun, which is usually about the spontaneous and the messy.

Anxiety about control, which can undermine self-confidence, often goes with rogue rules about responsibility which we can work to counter (see next section). Taking up creative activities which involve the unpredictable and the somewhat chaotic – such as painting, writing or pottery – can also ease off the brakes of control.

Fear of lack of competence

When women return to work after years spent at home rearing children, they frequently worry about their competence to do the job. It is often asserted by those who champion women returners that the skills required to manage a family and household are actually very similar to those required in the workplace. This is probably true. What's rather idealistically overlooked here though, is that the woman running a household is her own boss and may be able to vary her timetable to suit herself. In the workforce she will almost certainly have to adjust to being just one of a team, working to set hours and probably having to learn new skills such as operating a till, or a computer. She may also have initial worries about appropriate dress or working relationships.

Many of us worry about being competent enough, especially in front of our peers or superiors. This can lead us to behave in a compensatory manner: we may cram reports with every minute detail of relevant information, and fill our spoken presentations with heaps of facts and statistics that leave the audience dozing. Or perhaps we get fixated with acquiring qualifications which announce to ourselves and the world, that we are . . . competent!

Concern with competence often undermines confidence when we are tackling something unfamiliar, like a new job or project. Often, we would be wiser to concern ourselves with the *relevancy* of our message to other people, rather than be preoccupied with how competent our message makes us appear. We may find ourselves avoiding challenges such as improving our job prospects, learning new skills and meeting new people, because we're afraid of looking silly.

We can help ourselves by deliberately entering into situations where we have to learn and ask others for help. And if the very thought throws us into turmoil, well then we can practise in front of a mirror at home such alien phrases as 'I don't know anything about that', or 'I've no idea how to do this. Can you help me please?' Then, when you've actually made such an overture, don't waste precious time and emotion on agonising about your admission of ignorance; concentrate on learning the new skill.

When one of these fears affects our confidence, we often get anxious about the effect. We worry that we will be 'rumbled', that our need to feel approved and accepted, individual, in control or competent may be revealed. Our terrible secret will be out. So for instance, if I am secretly afraid of my lack of competence, and someone tries to offer me constructive criticism, then I will probably respond in a very touchy way. The next section offers a very effective way of conquering these fears.

CONFIDENCE TRICK: Learning from fear and failure

In this exercise, you are first going to identify how you can make constructive use of failure, and what fears, specifically, are holding you back. Then we shall go on to reduce them.

- Think of an incident where lack of confidence caused you to fail. Write down a description of it in the centre of a sheet of paper. Now have three routes leading to it, representing you, the other people involved and the situation. Describe along the routes how each one contributed to the incident.

- Pay special attention to the route representing *your* thoughts and behaviour. If similar circumstances were to occur again, what could you do differently? Could you have done anything differently to affect other people's behaviour and the situation? Write down your ideas as a pledge for future reference.

- Were any of the four fears I've just described: fear of isolation and rejection, fear of loss of identity, fear of loss of control and fear of lack of competence affecting how you thought and acted? Are you more familiar with one of these fears than the others? How does it make you think and act? Resolve to take your greatest fear – and don't worry, some of us experience all four, frequently – and to lessen its effect on your confidence. We shall now look at how to do this.

Self Talk and Rogue Rules

In situations where we feel confident, we don't think about it, and we're often unaware that we're feeling it. In situations where we *don't* feel confident, where we feel emotionally vulnerable and possibly physically ill at ease, our thoughts will be sabotaging us. These thoughts often take the form of beliefs or rules which run like a cassette tape through our minds; a form of self-talk which tells us how to respond, and which can cause us to think illogically and to be over-demanding of ourselves.

As good citizens and members of society, we must abide by rules, many of which oblige us to compromise between what we want as individuals, and what we need to do to live together in society. Many or our rules will have been learnt from our families and will have been created from specific religious and political beliefs. They will exert a very strong influence on how we live our lives, though we may not always be aware of this. My Welsh Baptist upbringing was preoccupied with the work ethic, with the result that I find it impossible to lie in bed late in the mornings – I believe that I should get up and work. This is very handy when I need the discipline to write a book, but a disadvantage when I'm exhausted and could really benefit from a lie-in. On the other hand, a friend of mine who had an Italian Catholic upbringing can't understand why I believe that work should take such precedence even over social and family matters. She believes that spending time with friends and family is much more important.

Often our rules act as strong pillars of support for our decisions, goals, and how we run our relationships. For instance, you may believe that people should treat one another with respect, that self-knowledge is important, that the disadvantaged in society should be supported by the advantaged. These are all useful rules which support us in our lives. Unfortunately, most of us operate 'rogue' rules, too; rules which are illogical and prevent us getting what we want. Rogue rules always involve the words: 'must', 'should', 'ought to', 'have to', or 'need to'. They also involve the word 'always'. Let me give you examples:

Fearing isolation and rejection, we may use rogue rules like: 'I must always put other people before myself', or 'Other people must always find me attractive', or 'The situation must always be calm'. These beliefs are of course unrealistically demanding – on ourselves, on others, and the situation.

If we worry about being overpowered by others, then we will use rogue rules like: 'I must always impose who I am on everyone else', and 'Other people will always want to threaten me', and 'The situation is always slightly dangerous and so I need to go on the offensive'. As we operate these rules we will be abrasive and aggressive to others.

When we have a strong fear of losing control, then our rogue rules will be: 'I must always take responsibility for everything that happens', and 'Other people always need me to organise them and sort them out', and 'The situation is always chaotic and it is up to me to impose some order'.

Anxiety about appearing competent also operates its rules: 'I should always achieve at everything I do', 'Other people will always be judging me very critically', and 'The situation always demands that I must do my very best'.

Identifying your rules

You can find the rules you use by asking yourself three questions and answering as honestly as you can:

1. What do I try hard to be?

2. What am I afraid of not being?

3. What do I absolutely not want people to discover I am?

Take some paper and a pen and describe or draw yourself in two different situations, one in which you felt confident and one in which you did not. Does the way you've depicted yourself bring to light any rules you were using? What messages were you giving yourself that began with 'I must be . . .'?

Rewriting your rules

There is one question we can ask of all our rogue rules and very rarely do. The question is: why? Why must you always achieve very highly, or take responsibility for everything? Why should everyone like you or treat you fairly? Why should the situation always be calm? When we look for solid evidence that our rogue rules are right, it becomes very difficult to find. Often, it is easier to find evidence to the contrary.

You will find it helpful to learn to challenge your rules. Take your, 'I must be . . .' messages and ask yourself, 'Why?' Then ask yourself, 'Always?' Then, 'In every situation?' and finally 'With all people?'

When you ask yourself 'why?' you may come up with the answer, 'Because I believe', when you mean, 'Because I know'. For instance, the rule 'All people must dislike me because I *believe* I'm bad', is not the same as 'Because I *know* I'm bad'. For your 'I knows', do you have concrete evidence that would stand up in a court of law? Or was it just something your parents or some other authoritative person told you? Determine to use *your own* rules, not other people's.

Rewrite your rules with, 'I'd prefer . . .', 'It would be better if . . .', 'I wish . . .', I expect . . .', and qualify them with 'buts'. For instance: '*I'd prefer* to cope with everything *but* it's unrealistic to expect to. I need support and time off during which I'm not held responsible.' And review your rules regularly in the light of new experience and information. For example, if you are making progress in your career and this involves you in very demanding work, you will need to be very selective about where and when you use a rule like: 'I'd prefer to achieve most of the time.' You will avoid stress if you stop using it at home and in your leisure time, for instance.

And treat yourself. If you identify what you know to be a very strong rogue rule that you put into operation a great deal – such as: 'I must be competent/liked/in control/highly individual', just take that one rule and for a whole day, every time you start to put it into operation, check your impulse. Forget about being competent in the supermarket, popular with your relatives, in control on the sports field, or highly individual in every meeting you attend. You could end the day feeling marvellously relaxed . . .

Here are some examples of how course participants have rewritten their rogue rules:

The nervous negotiator   Janice runs a successful design company, and generally her confidence is quite high. However, she gets 'in a terrible tizz' before any negotiation. She puts off making the phone call, and although she knows *how* to negotiate and it usually goes well, as she uses humour and flexibility, she still dreads it every time.

Janice worked out that she was using two rogue rules: 'I must never ever risk offending people', and 'Other people will always take it personally if I argue about money with them'. She changed these rules to: 'I'd prefer never to offend people . . . but sometimes inevitably I will', and 'Some people will take arguing about money personally, but in business, most won't'.

The anxious appraisee   David dreads his six monthly work appraisal interview with his manager. However it goes, he always feels sapped of confidence for several weeks afterwards. He responds very sensitively to any hint of criticism. He worked out that he was using the rogue rules: 'I should be competent all the time', and 'Other people must always be kind to me'. He more usefully rewrote these to become 'I'd like to be competent most of the time, but if I'm not, it's not the end of the world', and 'It would be preferable for people to be kind to me most of the time, but some people in certain situations just won't be'. His next appraisal was far less daunting and he reported enjoying thinking about and using his new rules.

The paranoid presenter   Sue is a medical rep and has to make frequent presentations to doctors. Following what she regarded as being a disastrous presentation, where the overhead projector had broken down and she had been asked some very tough questions, her confidence plummeted. Her anxiety, she felt was about these rules: 'I must always be in control', and 'Other people must always respect my authority'. Realistically, she rewrote them: 'I would like to be in control and as prepared as I can be, but in a situation like a presentation the unexpected will happen', and 'I will aim to make the majority of people respect me, but some won't'. Being much kinder to herself and more in touch with reality, her next presentation went very smoothly.

Rewriting your harshest rogue rules can be enormously helpful in realistically building your self-esteem and confidence. Let's now take a look at some further examples of using self-talk constructively.

Healthy Thinking

Healthy thinking helps us to keep matching our own perceptions of events and people with reality. We become more confident then, because we get confirmation back from the world that how we view things fits in with others' versions. We avoid that feeling that sometimes we get at parties or meetings when our confidence is low – that to everyone else we appear as if we're coming from another planet! Here are some guidelines for healthy thinking:

Don't dramatise   People rarely die as a result of suggestions being rejected, or fluffing a presentation or being discovered to have made a mistake. Sometimes however, we dramatise possible results of our behaviour with thoughts such as, 'It will be absolutely awful if people don't like what I suggest', or 'It will be dreadfully catastrophic if I'm found out to be less than competent'. Not so – you are likely to emerge intact in body and mind. Of course, catastrophes do happen, and if you have previously suffered abuse, violence or extreme bad luck, then thinking rationally about this will be of limited benefit; you may need to turn to professional help.

Your behaviour is not your identity If you have done something foolish, does it follow that you're a totally foolish person? I think not. You have *behaved foolishly on one occasion* (all right – on several occasions; who hasn't?). Recall all the occasions on which you have behaved wisely, to get a more balanced view.

The specific is not universal When other people are unfair to you occasionally, does it mean that all people are unfair – full stop? When the world treats you badly and causes you pain, does it mean that it will continue to do this for the rest of your existence? The answer to both questions is, of course – no. But if we expect these specific events to repeat themselves, then we can operate a self-fulfilling prophecy – ensuring that they will. Much better to take the: 'That's over and I have dealt with it; now I move on', attitude.

Avoid personalising everything As children, we regard ourselves as being at the centre of the universe, the cause of everything happening around us. As adults, some of us still cling on to this delusion. So when we go to a party, we expect everyone to be interested in us, and if they don't demonstrate this reaction, then we take this as evidence of some deficiency in ourselves. When we are using unhealthy thinking, we can take every reaction we get as evidence that confirms or disturbs our fragile self-image. So if the person we're talking to yawns, we take this as evidence that we are boring – allowing for no possibility that she or he may have had an exhausting day. When we personalise everything, all that happens to us is critical in defining who we are, because we are basically insecure. Well, some bad news I'm afraid, none of us is *that* important . . .

We can check whether we are the cause of the reaction, by asking people: 'Are you tired/all right/upset?' We can also be confident that in most situations people are more interested in pursuing their own agendas than in judging us critically.

Monitor your critical thinking   When we think critically, we examine ideas and argument, and consider alternatives. This is the basis of all intellectual activity, but we need to monitor our critical thinking, so that we don't habitually ask ourselves: 'What's wrong with this person/event/idea/my performance?' Otherwise, the admirable aspects of critical thinking can become an all pervasive negative attitude.

Keep your sense of humour   We can often increase our confidence in a situation by seeing ourselves and the other people involved in a humorous light. So see that intimidating audience as sitting there naked, that awkward questioner as a monkey and yourself as an irrepressible terrier. Let your imagination run riot and enjoy your private vision. It's a very creative way of healthy thinking and can give a useful perspective on people who are taking themselves too seriously.

Think with true discrimination   We human beings have an in-built tendency to categorise objects, places and other people. It's one way of making sense of the world. The trouble is that when we do this crudely, we become prejudiced. We stick a label on a group and all women become 'irrational'; all men become 'bad listeners'; all gays become 'a threat to the family', and all business leaders become 'greedy'. We then undermine our own confidence by becoming frightened of these 'aliens'.

As Ellen Langer points out in her book *Mindfulness*, when we do this, we are thinking with prejudice and without true discrimination. When we think in a discriminating way we look for shades of difference. Rather than lumping people together on the basis of just *one* shared similarity, we recognise that many women are highly rational, that many men are good listeners, that many gay women and men want to participate in family life, and indeed do, and that there are business leaders who possess a high sense of altruism and make valuable contributions to society.

This need for true discrimination is especially relevant when we are in contact with people who are disabled, or prejudiced against on the basis of skin colour and gender. Physically disabled people often find that people react to them as though they also have impaired mental functioning. Whereas, in fact, that man in a wheelchair may also be a father, an executive, an expert chess player, or an inventor. His disability, specifically, may be that he is unable to use his legs. Take this situation a little further and it could well be that until a few months ago he was as able-bodied as you or I, and is still struggling to come to terms with his changed situation. One sure thing is that whether a form of disablement is congenital or resulting from an illness or accident, the victim is entitled to the same courtesy and consideration we would wish for ourselves. The more we discriminate about who he is, the more we do him justice as a human being. Perhaps truly discriminating thinking is what political correctness should concern itself with, rather than a coy and overbearing preoccupation with the use of language.

Confidence, remember, is about confronting uncertainty. When we think with prejudice we don't do this – we simplify, reduce and deny complexity. When we truly discriminate and in doing so accept the massive variety and complexity of human beings, then we are thinking with true confidence.

Now on to another vital route to confidence: self-knowledge.

3 *Knowing Yourself*

CONFIDENCE KEY: How we interpret what happens to us, the roles we play, personality preferences

---

INSIGHT into 'who you are' is a most valuable resource in confidence building. Firstly, because it helps you appreciate just how uniquely individual each one of us is, and to be quite specific in identifying values that you share with others. Self-knowledge helps you understand that you may be using certain ideas to interpret events in ways which undermine your confidence. When you pinpoint these negative ideas, you can change them to something much more constructive, which builds your confidence.

Secondly, self-knowledge in terms of the roles you play (for example: daughter, wife and mother, and ambitious junior executive) helps you to identify how your confidence might be blocked by having too many or too few demands placed upon you. It helps you to see where and how you fit in with other people's roles, and helps you organise your life so that you can be as versatile or as single-minded as you choose.

Finally, with insight into our personalities and what we prefer, we can build our confidence by making the right choices in our interests and our careers. We can also use ideas about personality to help us understand that other people will have different preferences, and that these can sometimes cause misunderstandings. Our self-knowledge will help us understand more about others.

How We Interpret Events

Gillie came on a course with a rather odd problem. She said that she felt her confidence was being undermined by having to be part of a team at work. She worked as a researcher, and up until this point had been pretty much left to her own devices. She found the new system of team meetings and consultation very stressful. When Gillie examined what priorities she used in interpreting events, she found that independence was extremely important to her. If her independence was threatened, then she felt swamped. This was her overwhelming worry at the team meetings. Something else that Gillie regarded as very important was solving problems, and here she could see that a team approach might do this more effectively than an individual one. Gillie agreed that if she attended the meetings and consultation sessions, regarding them as an opportunity for solving problems, rather than as events where her independence was under threat, then she would feel more confident. She could shift her priorities and interpret events differently.

There are two key ways in which we interpret events:

1. We all have priorities or values through which we judge people and events and make sense of everything that happens to us.

2. We are all constantly engaged in comparing and contrasting, finding out how things are similar and different from one another. You may be reading this book for instance and register that it reminds you in some ways of similar books, while in other ways it takes a very different approach.

How do we identify our priorities? By recognising the values we use to judge people, objects and experiences. Take three people you know from a similar group: friends, or colleagues at work. Write down their names on a piece of paper – for ease of reference here I'll call them A, B and C. Which person do you prefer best? Let's suppose you decide upon A. What is it about this person that makes you like him or her particularly? Is he or she cleverer, kinder, more thoughtful to their friends; richer, funnier, more sensitive? Write down *your own* description, because this is about the way *you* see the world. The priority of the exercise is for you to express the description in a way that makes sense to you.

Now consider person B. How are they different from A and C? Again, write this down. Here you have another priority you use in judging people. And person C. How are they different from A and B? Here's your third priority.

When Gillie did this exercise, comparing three of her friends, she ended up preferring A, because she was self-possessed. Person B, compared with A and C was judged to be more clear-headed and decisive. And person C differed from A and B, by being extremely trustworthy. These three positive descriptions are important priorities Gillie uses when assessing people.

Psychology calls these priorities 'constructs'. Constructs are rather like metaphorical chopsticks floating around in our heads. They always have two ends, which describe values that are opposite in meaning. So Gillie's ideas about what she considers to be the opposite of her three priorities: self-possessed, clear-headed and decisive, and trustworthy could be clingy, muddle-headed and unreliable. When Gillie meets people then, it is as though she has these chopstick priorities floating around in her head. At the same time, she is wearing metaphorical spectacles, with those contrasting qualities built into the lenses, through which she 'sees' and interprets whatever happens to her, and whoever she meets. (See illustration on page 48.)

Take the three priorities you arrived at for interpreting your friends, and work out what your opposite values would be. It is your own meaning that's important – not a dictionary definition. You now have three constructs that *you* use as priorities for assessing people. If you want to find out more of the constructs that you use, then you could make some further comparisons, say, of three cars, places, holidays, fruit, restaurants – in exactly the same way in which you compared people.

Significant Measures

We will often find it easier to identify one end of a construct rather than the other. Let's say we consider relationships to be important. We may know that one way in which we measure our experience a lot of the time, is by how well our relationships seem to flourish. One end then of a significant measure for us would be:

relationships as important _____?

At the other end, some of us might put 'loneliness'; some of us might put 'getting tasks done'; and others might put 'looking after number

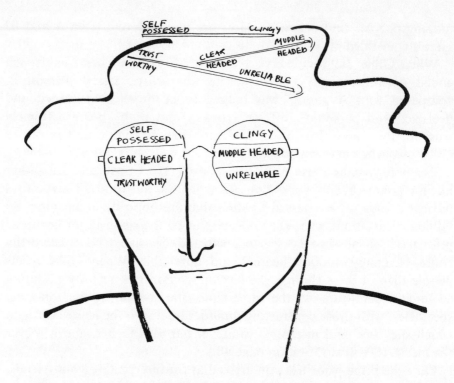

Gillie's Metaphorical Spectacles

one'. Through working hard to identify what less accessible contrasts we are using, we can learn a lot about how we interpret things.

Some of these metaphorical chopsticks will have been formed when we were babies. Some of them will have been formed through our experiences with families, friends and figures of authority. The sort of environment and opportunities we've been exposed to will also determine how we construct meaning. And our constructs will change in the light of new experience, so it is important that we view them as dynamic and changeable. This approach says that, above all, we are receptive researchers – constantly engaged in making sense of events and experimenting with our understanding of one another.

These ideas are exciting because we can apply them to everything that we do. For example, we can see people using constructs which begin with: 'I'm completely insignificant . . .' when they look drab or ill-groomed, and their conversation is monosyllabic and apologetic. In the context of confidence building these ideas are especially useful.

Let's say your confidence wanes whenever you have a job interview. Ask yourself: 'What is this situation about for me?' You may decide that an interview represents several constructs for you:

being judged harshly _____ **being thought well of**

prospect of failure _____ **certain of success**

interest in how they run interview _____ **no interest in interview**

Whenever you go for an interview, you find that 'being judged harshly' and the 'prospect of failure' dominate your mind. You make these constructs into questions and look for evidence that they are true, by sitting in the interview and asking yourself 'Is this interviewer judging me harshly?' and 'Am I being thought of as a failure?' Whereas you could approach the interview much more constructively by taking your third construct and turning that into your most crucial concern. Keep asking yourself: 'How are they running this interview?'

Some constructs, when used too much, can really damage our confidence. For example, we may be using a very dominant **superior ... inferior** construct, whereby virtually every situation we go into, we interpret in terms of how superior or inferior we are, compared to other people. We will find ourselves interpreting their behaviour entirely in terms of how it elevates us or puts us down. Or perhaps we make too much use of a construct such as:

other people's criticism ... other people's praise

and find ourselves constantly imagining that other people are disposed to be much more critical towards us than they actually are.

What we need to do is to find alternative constructs, that are more helpful towards building confidence. Like:

how I'm similar to others ... how I'm different

and

finding out about others ... being disinterested in others

We need to consciously use these constructs, rather than the less helpful ones. We can then stop self-destructive interpretations which lead us to be constantly involved in putting ourselves and others down.

CONFIDENCE TRICK: Constructs as Questions

We can help ourselves react more positively and with greater confidence in situations, by turning our constructs into helpful questions.

- Using the process as described above, take three situations. One where you were very confident (a), one where you were moderately confident (b), and one where you lacked confidence (c). What made situation (a) different from the other two? Make this into a construct with two opposite qualities at either end.

- How was situation (b) distinctive? Again, make a construct out of the two contrasting qualities the situation was about, for you. And what qualities make situation (c) different from the other two?

- Focus on situation (a). What questions did your construct cause you to ask yourself? For instance, using constructs like the ones described above:

how I'm similar to others . . . how I'm different

finding out about others . . . being disinterested in others

You could use helpful research questions like, 'What do I have in common with these people?' 'What makes these people tick?' You can use these helpful questions time and time again, to help keep your most supportive constructs uppermost in your mind.

Playing Roles

John is a computer specialist in his early forties. Having built a reputation for expertise as an employee in a large company, he now works as a freelance consultant. He has plenty of work, but one aspect of it bothers him:

'Just occasionally I get asked into a company where the whizz-kids in the department seem to doubt my expertise. They ask endless questions, which are often irrelevant. I feel that they're trying to trip me up, which undermines my confidence and I get irritated. I want to know why this is happening.'

When John talks about how he sees his role, it is very revealing. He sees himself as a boffin and an academic. His appearance and manner reinforce this: he favours corduroy jackets, and cardigans, and he speaks in an intense way. When John is asked to think about how *his clients* see him, he realises they expect him play the role of a management consultant. They expect him to present himself in a more business-like suit and to communicate with them so as to build a good working relationship, as well as getting on with the task in hand. John decides to embark on a programme of improving his self-presentation, so that he can be more adaptable in his role-playing.

Clarifying our roles

As Shakespeare wrote: 'All the world's a stage, and all the men and women are merely players.' All of us play roles to varying degrees in our lives. And as confidence is about building resources to deal with uncertainty, the clearer we are about these roles the better. Using the idea of role-playing, we can get insight into why confusion, lack of challenge and conflicting demands affect our confidence levels. We can choose to play roles so as to conform with, or to confound people's expectations of us, depending on what is most appropriate in any given situation.

How well we juggle our various roles will certainly influence the way our relationships with one another develop. We may have family roles, as parent, sibling, daughter, son; work roles, as supervisor, manager, executive, secretary; roles in society: woman, man, city-dweller, Greenpeace member and so on. We play our roles by means of our attitudes, our behaviour, the things we buy, where we live, how we look, the television programmes we watch and the books, magazines and newspapers we read. How we act, how we look and where we go are all to do with role-playing.

Role senders/role receivers

And all the time in our dealings with one another, we act not simply as role senders but as role receivers. Our children send us expectations of our roles as parents; our managers send us expectations of our roles as company employees. We send our partners expectations of how they should play their roles. Trouble can ensue when we or they contradict these role expectations. For example, the husband who fails to play the role of Prince Charming for his wife, wooing and protecting her, may end up in the divorce courts. Or the bank manager who decides to play the role of risk-taking entrepreneur with his customers' money and ends up in the job queue . . .

The more clearly our role is defined by other people, organisations and society, the less power we have to make our own decisions, to be creative, to live and work in a way we choose. We have to balance this against our needs to be accepted, to fit in and to live, work and prosper, with others. When organisations such as religious cults and large fast food chains or department stores give their followers and employees tightly prescribed rules for how they should behave and appear, they make these people more controllable and predictable.

CONFIDENCE TRICK: Role Call

Working out how many different roles you play can be an entertaining and enlightening exercise. It can make you realise just how versatile and responsible you, and others, expect you to be. It can also act as a helpful inventory to refer to, for cutting down on too much activity and responsibility, as described later in this chapter.

- List the roles you play, putting them into three categories: work, family and social roles. Be as imaginative as you like in your description. Ask yourself what do you do and who do you do it with, to or for? Here are some ideas:

Work: manager, slave, executive, guru, nanny, team-player, advisor, Ms Reliable, office clown.

Family: provider, mother, father, son, daughter, carer, rebel, social secretary, money machine, responsibility-taker, peace-maker.

Leisure: friend, reader, shopaholic, gourmet, gardener, charity worker, community activist, football fan, self-improver, aerobics fanatic.

Role Overload: Understudy Needed

Sometimes, we can find our confidence affected by just having too many roles and not enough resources such as money, time, energy and support from other people.

Jenny has taken a part-time job in a shop after several years at home bringing up children. She enjoys the work, doesn't find it particularly demanding, and especially likes meeting and dealing with the public. However, after a couple of months, something is nagging away at Jenny's confidence. She feels nervy in the shop and when she gets home in the evening, she feels exhausted and slightly depressed. She thinks it is something to do with the fact that the two other women who work in the shop with her do not get on well together and are constantly bickering. Jenny finds herself caught between the two of them.

When Jenny analyses her roles, she realises that as well as being a wife, mother, nurse, cook and cleaner, her new job involves her playing the role of saleswoman, too. She feels adequate to play all these roles. What she hadn't bargained for was the extra roles of counsellor and diplomat that her bickering colleagues are requiring of her. She resolves to talk this through with her colleagues and to explain that while she's happy with her saleswoman role, she is not happy with the other demands. She would like their help in making these obsolete, so that she can continue in the job. The bickering stops.

Reducing overload

Your confidence is eroded by role overload, because you feel torn in many directions and guilty about not playing all your roles effectively. You may feel undermined by not being able to be 'the perfect mother', 'the adoring wife', 'the corporate amazon', 'the good citizen' and 'the aerobics queen'. Yet common sense – and possibly your best friend – would tell you that it is a tall order you are trying to fill.

Unfortunately, we can't always relinquish some of these roles and thus lighten the load. But we *can* help ourselves build confidence by feeling effective in our most important roles. We need to review all the roles we play and select which ones are most important to *us*. This may mean flying in the face of social pressures and trends and deciding for instance that 'mother' is much more important, say, to us, than 'manager'.

Roles which other people foist on us, like Jenny's roles of 'counsellor' and 'diplomat' should either be low priorities for us, or discarded altogether.

It can be helpful to take your five most important roles, write them down in a column and then alongside write what you do in each role and what other people expect of you. Where there is a wide gap between what you do and what others expect, you may find it helpful to talk to those people about how they see your role and how you would like to play it. You can influence them so that they share more of your definition of your role (see Chapter Nine). The more we are able to choose what roles we play and how we play them, the more confident we will become.

Role Underload: Am I Really this Inadequate?

The roles we play change over time. Sometimes, we can find ourselves with too few roles and, lacking stimulation and motivation, we feel dissatisfied. Our confidence suffers, and we feel that we are isolated and have nothing to talk about with other people. This can happen to people who've been made redundant, parents at home with small children, or a mother whose grown-up children have recently left home. Or it may be someone who's changed jobs to something much less demanding; where they were used to playing lots of roles in their previous work, they find themselves playing just one or two.

But it isn't always having an insufficient number of roles that creates lack of confidence. We may be playing a role that is insufficiently demanding. This often happens to keen young graduates who join companies feeling ready to conquer the world and find themselves instead doing the filing for everyone else in the office, minding the photocopier and making the coffee.

Creating and expanding roles

If you lack confidence because of role underload, it's worth investigating new roles that you could take on. If your work roles are insufficiently stimulating and alternative prospects of work are bleak, then you could look at ways to increase your social roles. More and more people today are getting involved in community groups and activities. You might like to get more actively involved in charity work, an environmental campaign, or a personal development group. Perhaps the role of 'student' appeals and you could take up part-time study, for the sake of interest or to further your career.

You could also work to persuade your boss that you can take on more, and thereby contribute more to the organisation. Show an intelligent interest in what is going on around you – and *read* that filing when you have time. It could give you an overview of the whole department – invaluable if a vacancy does arise. Be persistent with your ideas and suggestions. If your immediate boss dislikes your enthusiasm (perhaps because it's threatening to his or her position) other people will notice and approve.

There is a lot of evidence to suggest that many people have too little scope to expand and innovate in their roles at work. Forward looking organisations who give their employees this scope, will benefit in business terms. Experiments at the Harvard Business School proved this to be the case.

In the first experiment, actors performing a play were asked to act their parts with as much novelty as possible. The audience were then asked to rate the actors for charisma. In the second part of the experiment, the actors were asked to perform their roles as closely as they could to the script. The audience then again rated them for charisma. Not surprisingly, the first ratings for charisma were much higher than the second. The actors were valued for being creative and innovating in their roles.

A second experiment involved two groups of encyclopaedia salesmen. The first group was told to approach every customer as if he or she was their very first customer. They needed to respond spontaneously to everything that happened, and to be as adaptable as possible. The second group was to be as consistent as possible in dealing with all customers.

Both groups were again rated by their customers for charisma, and, as in the previous experiment, the first group scored much higher than the second. Its members were also regarded as being more expert, having more impact and being more persuasive. Presumably, they would have sold more encyclopaedias.

Where customer and client contact is important then, expansion and innovation in role-playing should be encouraged. This is an approach that can boost business and confidence, and help organisations to keep their brightest and best people.

Role Clarity

Confusion about roles can mar confidence. If you're unsure about what is expected of you, or you have to answer to too many people, then uncertainty will cause your confidence to plummet. Jane has this problem:

Jane is a secretary, and her boss, Anna, is easy-going and vague. She has told Jane she expects her to just 'generally look after me'. Anna works alongside two other managers – Steve and Helen – and they all share a large open-plan office. Jane finds herself being given orders and work to do by both Steve and Helen, when their own secretaries can't cope. Sometimes, they insist that their demands must take priority over work Jane is doing for Anna, because, 'It's an urgent need for the whole department.' Jane feels confused and insecure quite a lot of the time.

Using assertiveness skills (see Chapter Eight) Jane asks Anna to describe how she sees Jane's role. And what exactly she expects and needs in terms of priorities. Anna gives Jane much clearer guidelines for what needs to be done, when and what work she can refuse to do. As a result, Jane feels more confident generally, about her job.

We vary greatly as to the extent to which we interpret our roles to be about task or relationship; that is, about getting the job done or working well with and through people. Ideally, you should aim to strike a balance. If you view your role as being mainly about the job in hand, as John did at the beginning of this section, then you may overlook people's feelings and responses. If you become over-preoccupied with your role in terms of relationships, then you may be diverted from achieving the task.

If you are unclear about a role, you will find it useful to describe that role under two column headings: What I do (tasks) and Who I do it with or for (relationships). Once you've listed your tasks and relationships, you will be much clearer about the aspects that you would like to improve and develop.

CONFIDENCE TRICK: Ideal Role

- Help yourself to achieve what you want in the future, by picturing yourself in your ideal role. What would your tasks be in that role? What sort of relationships with others would you have and who would these people be? What would they expect from you? How would you look and sound? How would you think and feel? Where would you be?

- Write down all these ideal facets of your future life and keep this record as a confidence booster, for times when you get disheartened. Once you have clarified your ideal role in this way, it will help you to attain your goals. It will become a lot easier to work towards what you want, and strange as it may seem, with this strong image in your mind, opportunities will often present themselves.

Personality Preferences

Our confidence grows when we have clear ideas about what we like and don't like, and can use these preferences to shape our ambitions and make decisions. We can also better understand how they sometimes act as limitations.

Psychometric tests, which analyse personality and predict how people will behave, are popular tools to help personnel and training staff in selection, assessment and development. The underlying assumption behind these tests is that we can be categorised into types and that these types remain relatively stable. From the point of view of the people *giving* the tests, they can be very useful. Rather than having to rely entirely on their own judgement to select new employees, the test can do it for them. If an error is made, then the test can be blamed. So personnel staff can also use tests to boost their confidence.

From the point of view of the person *taking the test*, if the results are explained constructively then the findings can be useful. However, you may disagree vehemently with the results, and they may make you more certain that you *know* who you are, better than any so-called 'scientific' test. Or the results may confirm things you already knew about yourself, and give you constructive suggestions for the future. They may prevent you from trying to be a square peg in a round hole. You could find the test results provide a useful starting point for further self-examination, and help in making career choices.

On the discount side, once we've been categorised in such a test, we may be tempted to use the 'diagnosis' as an excuse: 'Well, I know I caused offence by being so opinionated, but what do you expect, I'm an extrovert.' And we can use the 'findings' to put off change: 'Well I've always been a blushing introvert. It's too late for me to do anything about it now – that's how I am.'

The thinking behind this, is that we can't change. It is a very defeatist attitude. And there is much evidence to suggest otherwise. Have you changed in the last five years? I certainly know that I have. Of course we can all learn, change and develop. And these changes are likely to be most effective when they start from a base of self-knowledge about what we already prefer.

Probably the best-known of the psychometric tests is the Myers-Briggs test. According to Isabel Briggs Myers, one of the developers of the test, we do not change our basic preferences, but we can make ourselves more adaptable, aware of our resources and how to use them and, therefore, more confident.

Most studies of types of people, including the Myers-Briggs, are based on Carl Jung's ideas about people having different preferences, as detailed below. Have a look at these and see if you can identify yourself:

Extroversion and Introversion

Eleanor and Sam are discussing a friend, Tim. They both agree that Tim is a drama queen, plunging from one crisis to another, the lurid details of which he regales them with, at length, on the phone. Eleanor finds Tim's accounts exhausting, while Sam finds them exhilarating and usually recounts dramatised versions to his office colleagues.

These preferences are about where we get energy and meaning from. Extroverts prefer external reality, the reactions of other people endorse their self-image. Extroverts often think aloud. They will seek stimulation: eating, watching television, talking and reading – sometimes all at once. Because other people give them energy, their confidence may be affected by separation from others, and by isolation. This could be occasioned, say, by the promotion that puts them in an office apart from their team; or the redundancy that makes them lonely and solitary.

It has been suggested that balancing our preferences can make us happier; that developing introvert skills of thinking, listening, reflection and contemplation will give extroverts greater resources for dealing with confidence crises (see Chapter Four).

Introverts, in contrast, prefer internal reality. Clarity, order and achievement endorse who they are. Introverts may be so busy thinking and listening that they make very little contribution to discussion, so wrapped up are they in their world of ideas. They will seek to quietly recharge themselves after spending a lot of time with people. Because order, clarity of thinking and achievement give them confidence, chaos and a lot of unpredictable stimulation may undermine it.

Developing extrovert social skills of making small talk effectively, interrupting and expressing a viewpoint, can help the introvert to build confidence in the external world (see Chapter Seven).

CONFIDENCE TRICK: Understanding People

- If someone regularly saps your confidence, could it be that, with your extrovert tendencies, you are disturbing their enjoyable solitude? Or, if you have introvert tendencies, are you making them feel isolated, or excluded? Where the relationship is important to you, you may want to temper your outgoing tendencies or self-contained introspection to show consideration for the other person's preferences.

CONFIDENCE TRICK: Job Satisfaction

- Extroverts will enjoy contact with lots of people during working hours. Introverts will enjoy working alone. If your job doesn't match your preferences, can you find ways of satisfying them during your leisure time?

Sensing and Intuiting

A married couple, David and Beth, are at a dinner party. Beth starts to relate a funny incident that happened to the couple while on holiday. She describes in detail the build up to a misunderstanding with a camel driver, Ahmed. She also describes Ahmed's personality, and what motivates him. David constantly contradicts her account with: 'It wasn't like that, darling', 'You're exaggerating wildly', 'What about the facts?' and 'He didn't think that about us!!!'.

These differences indicate the way we take information in from the world around us. Jung defined sensation as: 'Telling you that something exists', and people who prefer sensing like tangible facts and details. They prefer to use what they can see, hear, touch, taste and smell as their means of gathering information. Having to deal with too many theories and abstractions, may cause the person who prefers sensing to lose confidence. Like David, sensors can limit themselves by being over-fixated with facts and minute details and not seeing the big picture. They can lose a sense of priority and context.

Sensors can make themselves more adaptable by exercising their imaginations a little more. In the story above, perhaps the details and facts are not that important, in terms of entertainment value. Beth, the intuitive partner, is intent rather on telling a good story.

Jung defined intuition as: 'Telling you whence something came from and where it is going.' People who prefer to intuit, use the information they get from their senses, to create connections and possibilities and to find hidden meanings. Details, deadlines and definite time-spans can sap the intuitive's confidence. Intuitives can limit themselves by being *too* theoretical, so that what they are considering and suggesting seems to be of little practical relevance.

To become more versatile, it is worth while for those of us who prefer intuitive responses to sometimes just experience what is happening at face value, without searching for deep and hidden meaning.

CONFIDENCE TRICK: Understanding People

If you are a sensor and you want to communicate effectively with an intuitive, could you contribute a few abstract ideas along with your fact-based suggestions? Vice versa, as an intuitive, can you provide your sensor with tangible facts and concrete details?

CONFIDENCE TRICK: Job Satisfaction

If you are a sensor considering a career change, does your ideal job give you an opportunity to deal with the concrete and immediate and use practical skills? As an intuitive, can you consider the overview and make connections between thoughts and people, in the new job?

Thinking and Feeling

The joint heads of a department have been told they have to lose a member of staff. Jill wants to discuss the situation and use criteria such as how long people have been in the department to make the decision. Alan wants to lose Sally, who he knows has been unhappy in her job and has had other offers. Both Jill and Alan are adamant that their approach to the decision is the 'right' one. These distinctions are most concerned with decision making. Jung's use of language was slightly confusing here, because people who show a preference for thinking also feel, and vice-versa. The thinking description actually refers to people like Alan, who wants to make decisions in a highly objective, detached and analytical way. They can make decisions impersonally, with the fairness of the decision more of a concern than its effect on people. A tendency to not worry about taking unpopular decisions may mean that they sometimes overlook people's feelings when their response is important. They also fail to consider that if people feel strongly about a decision, they may sabotage it. Learning to ask others about their emotional responses can often make people who express this preference more confident about their ability to communicate.

People like Jill, who take feeling decisions, are much more concerned with how the decision will affect people's feelings, and with harmony and involvement. They are likely to be more subjective about making decisions. A tendency to get over-involved in the emotional temperature of events, may mean that sometimes they need to work hard at standing outside and keeping an objective overview. Learning to depersonalise conflict will be helpful in building confidence.

CONFIDENCE TRICK: Understanding People

- **Thinking too hard? Then try to give a little more attention to how others may *feel*. Over-sensitive to emotional responses!? Then analyse! analyse! analyse! Are you letting your sensitivity to others cloud your judgement?**

CONFIDENCE TRICK: Job Satisfaction

With a thinking preference, can you work where you do lots of planning and objective decision making? With a feeling preference, does your role involve creating good relationships between people?

Judging and Perceiving

Sandra and Helen are going shopping in their lunch hour. Sandra works out a plan of the shops they should visit, and what she wants from each. Helen is put out. For her, shopping should be about a leisurely stroll around wherever she likes the look of. And, who knows, *perhaps* she'll decide to buy something . . .

These differences are about how we relate to the world through what we say and do. People who show a preference for judging, use decision making to drive their lives: planning, ordering and controlling. Their work and leisure times will be structured. Confidence crises can arise when these people become too rigid about their decisions and ignore new and important information. So the message is: loosen up.

People who prefer perceiving, in contrast, keep collecting information, and prefer an easy-going, open-minded approach to the world. They are less likely to be quick to make decisions or take stands on issues. Confidence crises can arise when nothing gets finished. So in such cases, the message is: set goals and realistic deadlines for at least one or two projects, and try to keep to them.

CONFIDENCE TRICK: Understanding People

- If you're communicating with a person who prefers judging, can you get shape and order into your ideas? With someone who prefers perceiving, can you suggest spontaneity and impulse?

CONFIDENCE TRICK: Job Satisfaction

- Some companies and jobs are much more about order, structure and punctuality than others; if your preference is for judging, this will suit you. A more informal, unpredictable environment will be better for you, if you are a perceiver.

Here ends our trip along the route of self-knowledge. Now we move into another dimension altogether, and one that increasing numbers of people are turning to, in order to give their lives meaning: the spiritual approach.

4 *The Spirit of Confidence*

CONFIDENCE KEY: Building inner confidence via alternative therapies

' A SELF-REALISED being is somebody with a supreme self-confidence and self-esteem, but with total lack of ego. Such a being is somebody who has a purpose in life, who can connect to all living things, who can look on other people with unconditional love but with detachment and respect. A fully realised individual does not seek after material, sensual pleasures or worldly fame, but has gained immense strength by being able to get in touch with their innermost being.' Liz Hodgkinson, *The Personal Growth Handbook*.

Today, more and more people are turning towards alternative ideas and therapies to make themselves feel better about their health, their attitude towards life, and their relationships with others. Books and workshops describe how to use these ideas to heal yourself from illness, make more money, or even to completely reinvent yourself. And the description 'alternative' coves a wide-ranging collection of beliefs and practices, including colonic irrigation, crystal gazing, meditation, and self-healing.

Using alternative approaches to tend to your spirit can help build confidence. Irma is an advisor to small businesses:

'A couple of years ago, my confidence really dropped. And I couldn't work out why. On the surface I had everything that our society regards as badges of success: my own very successful business, a happy family and a lovely home. But I felt something was missing. I was rushing around living life at a frantic pace, almost in order to avoid myself. I felt nervous and insecure a lot of the time. I wasn't sure that my life had any meaning. A friend suggested that perhaps I should think about

64

my spiritual life – that perhaps I needed to look inwards and work towards an inner sense of peace. She suggested I look at various "alternative" ideas.

'I took up meditation and although I found it very difficult to begin with, I soon felt much more, well, "centred". I felt peaceful deep in my mind. I found myself thinking about my values and decided I wanted to do something where I could use my skills a bit more to help others. So, I delegated the running of my original business to my very able staff and I became a small business advisor. I find this very rewarding – helping others to grow – and I'm feeling much more fulfilled. My confidence has returned.'

An Holistic Approach

Alternative approaches to personal development and confidence-building, are usually based on certain values and beliefs which it is useful to be aware of. If you have just read the chapter on self-knowledge, then you will appreciate that your preferences will affect your response to alternative ideas. The values and beliefs behind these ideas include an emphasis on the importance of your experience as an individual, and what it means to you. And as an individual you are regarded holistically, that is, with mind, body and soul as an integrated whole. Alternative thinking often suggests that personal transformation – changing ourselves as individuals – will lead to global transformation, changing the world for the better.

These approaches often suggest, too, that every live thing on the planet is connected via energy and the 'life force'. They incorporate ideas from Eastern religions such as Hinduism and Buddhism. They place more emphasis on intuition and feeling than on the rational and the logical. This doesn't mean, however, that 'intuition' and 'logic' are opposed to one another; they are just different types of thinking and response.

However, we should not regard alternative approaches as offering a complete cure-all to our troubles, nor should we allow unscrupulous gurus to exploit us. Neither should we completely dismiss these ideas as being opposed to conventional or established viewpoints. These days increasing numbers of scientifically trained doctors and psychologists are investigating alternative therapies, and suggesting them to their patients and clients as an adjunct to established methods.

Alternative ideas also offer some powerful techniques for confidence building. In conventional medicine, the placebo effect of pills is well-researched: given a dummy pill, many of us will report an improvement in our condition. The same applies with some of the more eccentric new age therapies. If we believe, for instance, that talking to crystals is going to build our confidence, and we want it to happen enough, then the strength of our belief may make us feel better. Some of what I consider to be the wiser therapies, such as aromatherapy and the Alexander technique, will be referred to in later chapters on stress control and appearance. Here I want to look at techniques concerned more directly with building confidence in our minds and spirits.

A Personal Philosophy

Quite recently, a friend of mine died, following a long illness. She approached her death with what seemed to me to be considerable confidence. She knew she was dying, and although she had moments of great fear and despondency, her suffering eventually became so great that she wanted to die. At her funeral, carefully planned by her beforehand, readings from Kahlil Gibran's *The Prophet* and the New Testament, spelt out to her friends and relatives her spiritual beliefs. The readings spoke of the importance of love, and how much life and death were connected. They spoke of how we would all meet again, later. Though not a practising Christian, my friend had strong spiritual beliefs concerning the connectedness of all things, and the after-life. These beliefs gave her confidence when she faced her greatest test.

If we ignore our spiritual needs, then we may also lack a sense of purpose in life, and have no profound sense of why we are here. We may, without realising it, be very afraid of death. We will avoid thinking and talking about the subject. We will lack confidence.

Without realising it too, in overlooking our spiritual needs, and avoiding thinking about death, we will affect the way we live. We may 'live for the moment' and think that death won't happen to us, that we are immortal. This way, we can live life in the fast lane, taking risks and seeking short term high rewards. Or we may live our lives by plodding along as if we have centuries to go. Living tortoise lives, we may put everything off until another day, another year.

Or we may simply follow religious beliefs that we got from our families, without questioning them. These beliefs may say we should suffer on earth and that our reward will come in heaven. We may live our lives accepting underdog status, and never doing anything about it, with a sense of passive hopelessness. Or we may be attracted to a cult religion, of the kind used to control people, and in which it is in the vested interest of those people in power to nurture our unquestioning acceptance. We then become completely controllable. We are encouraged to think in black and white terms: other creeds have nothing to offer us and are to be regarded as threatening.

So how do we avoid such traps and acquire a personal philosophy, a spiritual strength? Well, it's often a lonely quest. Such matters embarrass people. We are all dying from the moment we are born, yet the majority of us conspire silently not to talk about such a subject. Avoid it, and it will go away. Outside of university philosophy departments, few of us are comfortable talking about the meaning of life. So we need to embark initially on a research project, exploring ideas through reading books on related subjects, through attending religious services, or through going to workshops and meeting people who are on a similar quest.

Events that stand out in our lives will also shape our personal philosophy. Thinking back over significant events in your own life, have they made you draw any philosophical conclusions of your own?

Home Alone

Sometimes, we lack confidence through being afraid of solitude and loneliness. We don't want to have time to think, to have to deal with troubling ideas that we can avoid while we're busy being with others. We don't feel comfortable at the prospect of looking inside ourselves, and of facing our weaknesses and shortcomings. At a recent psychology conference, a researcher investigating people's fears, said that the fear of loneliness was the most widespread.

As we live in a world where successful people promote themselves outwards, through their appearance and performance in the various media, we could think that confidence is all about image projection. Though this aspect is important, if we want widespread recognition, it cannot bring the deeply held sense of confidence that comes from a calm spirit. Here's Anna, a management consultant talking about an experience she had:

'This sounds daft, but the other day I had this kind of revelation in

Sainsbury's car park, of all places. I was sitting in the car, and just realised all of a sudden that I was very lonely. I felt very emotional and wept for quite a while in self-pity. Rather than driving off immediately and putting my mind to something else, which would be my usual reaction, I stayed where I was – just sitting in the car – and continued to think about loneliness. I realised that loneliness is something I have to learn to live with. It goes with my demanding and successful career – it's part of the choice I've made about how I live my life. But I've resolved to make more of a conscious effort to keep in touch with friends, rather than always leaving them to call me. More importantly I think, I've decided to make better use of my time alone – to read, to relax, to write or to paint – rather than moping about because I don't have a husband and children, like most women of my age. Goodness knows what anyone who saw me wailing away in the car park thought, but afterwards, I felt much calmer, as though I'd confronted something I needed to.'

As individuals, we vary considerably in how much time we need to have alone, and as to when the bliss of solitude becomes the burden of loneliness. If you are always frantically rushing around, if family and friends seem to place great demands on your time, or if you find yourself desperately filling in your diary with social events so that you never spend time by yourself, then it could be some creative solitude is just what you need. Having time to think, reflect and plan is restorative and for many of us, essential to our confidence.

When you are very busy, then it is useful to make the most of what little time you have for solitary activities. One of the best ways to do this, is through meditation.

Meditation: Maharishi Magic

Meditating doesn't mean necessarily sitting cross-legged in a painful position with a transcendent expression on your face, and endlessly sighing 'om ... om ...'. It can be done in any position, and in my opinion, there is no great mystique to the technique, although people who run expensive courses on meditation might tell you otherwise.

The benefits of meditation, and other mind calming techniques are scientifically validated. When awake, our brains produce three types of waves: beta, theta and alpha. Beta waves are activated when our brains are working hard, absorbing information and solving problems. Theta waves are activated when we are drowsing, or feeling emotional. Alpha waves are activated when we are relaxed, but also aware and receptive; they are also associated with pleasurable experiences and with creativity. Researchers have found that people who meditate regularly, have high levels of alpha wave production.

Meditation is a kind of mind clearing which, performed regularly, can help to create calmness and confidence. In my experience, it can recharge the mind so as to enable the meditator to return to work, thoroughly refreshed. And all in return for setting aside twenty minutes a day to practise this art.

CONFIDENCE TRICK: Mantra Power

To mediate effectively, you first of all need to be able to relax physically. There are two popular methods of relaxation, which you may well be familiar with.

- The first involves working through the body part by part, starting with the toes, clenching them, then releasing them, so that they are relaxed. Then move up to the ankles, calves and so on. Take your time so that you thoroughly relax each part of your body before moving on to the next one.

- The second method involves visualising yourself some- where very pleasant and relaxing, such as a beach, a meadow or a cool white room. Keep this picture in your mind, and all the accompanying sensations that go with it: the sound of waves, the smell of grass, or gentle, rhythmic tick of a clock, until you feel relaxed. (New age tapes of sounds, music and descriptions of scenes are now widely available in book shops and health food shops. You may want to try one or more of them.)

- If you are tired, and therefore likely to fall asleep when you meditate, sit, rather than lie down. If you do lie down, place a cushion or pillow behind your head, and lie with your knees bent and as much of your back as possible flat on the supporting surface.

- Become aware of your breathing. You may find it helpful

to think about breathing in calmness or relaxation, and breathing out tension or anxiety. If your breathing seems jerky and rushed, just sigh out slowly and gently several times as you breathe out.

- Now focus on your mind and let it fill with space, or white light. Krishnamurti, the Indian philosopher, said meditation was freedom from thought. If a thought intrudes, simply observe it, and let it float away. Keep returning your attention to the clear space or white light. Stay like this until you feel well rested. If you find it difficult to focus on space or white light, instead, concentrate on a pool of restful colour – deep green or blue, perhaps.

- Some people like to repeat a word or sound when they meditate. You might want to use 'rest' or 'easy' or 'calm', for instance.

- When you've finished, take your time to get up gently and walk around slowly, to restore the circulation.

People have reported all sorts of sensations and experiences during meditation. Although it may feel extremely restful, it is definitely not the same as sleep. If you are sleeping, you are not meditating. If you do doze off, don't get disheartened. Next time, try when you do not feel so tired, perhaps at a different time of the day. And do try to practise regularly, preferably in the same place. Try to choose a time and place when and where you are not likely to be disturbed.

Meditating on space is said to improve intuitive powers. It's as though you are creating lots of space in your mind, so that leaps of connection can be made. If you want to improve your concentration, then focusing on a simple shape such as a circle, square or triangle is said to be effective. If your attention wanders, simply draw it back. At first you may have to do this very often, but don't give up. Your concentration will improve if you persevere.

Realistically, if you can meditate three or four times a week for fifteen to twenty minutes, you should soon feel some benefits. Faced with something that challenges your confidence – a job interview, or a speech perhaps – allow yourself some time to meditate before setting out. In addition to calmness and confidence, you may find that the technique helps you to come up with unexpected answers to problems.

Experienced meditators become able to use the technique even in crowded tube trains. If the subject interests you and you would like to study it further, please see the reading list for this chapter.

Visualisation: I Have a Dream . . .

Martin Luther King's famous words began one of the most moving and inspiring speeches ever. Like other great orators, he tapped into our collective dreams. Each one of us also has our own individual dreams and visions, and they are a valuable part of our identity.

Visualisation is a technique whereby we use the power of our imagination to create possibilities. Unlike meditation, where the aim is to rest from thought; in visualisation, we deliberately conjure up images. Advertisers use the power of visualisation all the time: we see ourselves drinking Bovril and looking like Jerry Hall (but perhaps not in the chicken outfit she wore in the advertisement); we see ourselves drinking Gold Blend and our sex lives improving dramatically . . . if only.

Today, visualisation is used in all sorts of contexts: from helping people cope with and perhaps recover from serious illness to sports coaching. Businesses sometimes use it as part of organisation development: to explore possibilities and potential for the future. Research seems to suggest it can work. An American university took three groups of evenly matched golf-players. The first group was asked to visualise themselves improving their game. The second group was asked to visualise their game gradually deteriorating. The third group (the control group) was given no instructions about the game. The groups were surveyed over a period of time. In the first group, which had been using positive visualisation, performance improved by an average of 30 per cent. In the second group, using negative visualisation, performance worsened by 21 per cent. The control group had improved by 10 per cent.

In confidence building, we can use visualisation in several ways:

CONFIDENCE TRICK: Undoing the Past

Visualisation can be used to lessen the impact of the past, if you've had a bad experience which has affected your confidence.

- Relax yourself physically, and play the experience back in your mind's eye. Picture yourself very clearly at the end of the experience.

- Now replay it, with you emerging at the end of the experience, unscathed. See yourself walking away from the event, in jaunty fashion, and while the event becomes blurred, the image of you with your confidence intact will become larger and more sharply defined. Hold on to that image and remember it, so you can recall it immediately when you need a boost.

CONFIDENCE TRICK: Forward to the Future

Relax yourself physically by using one of the techniques described in the Meditation section.

- Now think of a situation where you would like to have more confidence. Visualise yourself in the situation, behaving as you do at present. How do you look, sound, feel?

- Then play the situation again, only this time you are there as a confident person. How do you look, sound and feel this time? What do you say? Keeping this image of yourself in your mind's eye, you will find it helpful – and good fun – to get up gently and walk around the room behaving in the manner of this confident image of yourself. Get comfortable with this confident behaviour, so you can use it again, on demand.

- Whenever you've got something daunting coming up, such

as an interview or appraisal, visualise yourself dealing with it in a confident manner and feeling good about it afterwards.

Time for vision

Andrew Ferguson, who runs workshops at the Breakthrough Centre in London has an enlightening approach to time management. He suggests we start each day by giving some priority time to our personal dream, whether it is to write a novel, be more relaxed or to be more fulfilled in relationships. Though we all have long term visions for ourselves, we often do little about them. Other, more mundane matters, intrude. Andrew suggests that, even if it does mean getting up earlier, we give ourselves an extra hour in the morning to write, to relax or to organise more of a social life. This way we feel more satisfied and get closer to fulfilling our personal dreams.

I used to be less than entirely convinced about the power of visualisation. A few years ago, though, I went to a workshop run by Gill Edwards, who writes about and teaches visualisation techniques. In the workshop we were encouraged to visualise something we would really like to happen within the next six months. At that time, I was very keen to work in television, so in my visualisation I saw myself being filmed for a series. Three months later the BBC asked me to write and present a series on confidence building. Coincidence or proof – who knows? . . .

Affirmations and Self-fulfilling Prophecies

Affirmations are another popular New Age practice. We are the recipients of affirmations from many sources: 'Take this pill and it will make you better.' 'Buy this cosmetic and it will take ten years off your life.' 'Take out this insurance policy and enjoy peace of mind.' To build confidence, we can use them as self-talk, as uplifting messages that boost our belief in ourselves. Affirmations are brief positive statements, that need to be repeated regularly. We can use them to counter rogue rules, and to build confidence. So, for instance, as someone who finds meeting strangers daunting you might find it useful to repeat the phrase: 'Every day I'm getting more confident about meeting people.' Affirming this phrase frequently to yourself will only work though, if you've identified that you give yourself other messages like: 'Other people might overpower me', or 'Other people must like me', which do not serve you well. Positive affirmations work rather like tape recordings – we can erase an old, negative message by recording over them with positive, new ones.

Research experiments in social psychology show that we often create our own self-fulfilling prophecies through negative self-talk. We give ourselves negative messages, such as: 'You'll be lonely if you move', or 'You're not good enough to get through this interview', or 'You can't stand up for yourself against aggressive people'. Whether these messages are accurate perceptions of reality or not, they reinforce our uncertainty and diminish our confidence even further.

The best way to use affirmations, I think, is to gather them from your own experience. Keep them short and simple. For example, following an especially warm phone call with your partner, remind yourself: 'I am loved.' When a presentation goes well, or someone writes or phones to thank you for something, tell yourself: 'I am appreciated', or 'I am valued.' On successfully completing a challenging project, endorse your pleasure with: 'I have achieved something to be proud of.' A store of affirmations based on real experiences, such as these, can serve us well and help put things into perspective. What does failing your driving test matter, when set against affirmations like: 'I am loved'?

To work, affirmations need to give positive encouragement, to turn our fears and negative beliefs into constructive messages: 'I'm worried about failing', will become: 'I'm likely to succeed.' Or, 'I'm not very good at this', becomes: 'I'm quite good at this.'

Every time we tackle something challenging, we should reward ourselves at the end with some positive affirmations about what we did well. That is not to say we should ignore where there is room for improvement. But a bank of positive affirmations is a tremendous resource for increasing confidence.

Believing in Abundance

There is one other aspect of New Age or alternative philosophy that is worth mentioning here. This is what's called 'abundance thinking' or 'prosperity consciousness'. In the first chapter of this book, I talked about possible risks in becoming confident; one of them being that some of our contacts may become jealous. When people envy the confidence of others it is because they feel they lack that quality themselves and that *confidence is in limited supply*. Now this is clearly not the case. /An abstract quality like confidence is infinite in its supply; we can all tap into it if we so wish.

The same can apply to power and money. But many of us believe that power and money are in limited supply and so we must jealously guard our resources of them. Our beliefs about availability and how abundant a resource is, play a very strong role in our attitudes: 'As any economist will confirm, money magically expands and contracts according to people's confidence levels. When we feel positive and abundant the economy is buoyant. When we collectively feel fearful and limited the economy sinks' (Gill Edwards). Certainly, the past decade in Britain seems to confirm this. Business confidence – the belief that prosperity is possible and that money is in plentiful supply, declined dramatically – and so did the economy.

When we believe that resources such as confidence, money, power and love are in short supply, and that we are likely to be deprived of them, we can become preoccupied with self-denial and scrimping. We won't allow ourselves to enjoy any of these resources, because the risk of losing them seems so great. We need to take great leaps of faith, to allow ourselves to believe that there *is* abundance of much of what we want in the world. Risking our pride on the outcome of a relationship, or our pocket in investing in a course we really want to take, may well bring us great returns in the long term.

Scientists know remarkably little about how the brain works. No-one has proved irrefutably that we have an unconscious or subconscious mind, that intuition exists, that we cannot transfer thoughts to one another. The links between our minds and bodies, while acknowledged, need far more research. For anyone interested in what makes themselves and other people tick and confidence building, alternative ideas are certainly worth exploring.

5 *Getting Motivated*

CONFIDENCE KEY: Goal setting, learning from others, satisfying your needs

JIM is a non-fiction writer: 'My first book was agonising to write. I had thousands of ideas in my head but the first draft was a complete shambles. A helpful editor advised me that it lacked direction – did I have any idea what the goal of writing the book was? And had I considered that each chapter should take the reader progressively nearer to that goal? This was like a light suddenly going on in my head. I restructured my mountains of content, and threw out anything that wasn't strictly relevant to the direction of the book. I'm pleased to say that it sold very well indeed, and that still, ten years later, almost every time I sit down to write at my computer, I remember and am grateful for that editor's advice. She gave shape to my motivation.'

Undoubtedly, one of the best ways to gain confidence is to make things happen, for ourselves and for others. To feel effective is a great boost, and we can reflect upon our past effectiveness when the going gets rough. When we make things happen, it encourages us to keep trying, to have a sense of purpose and direction in life, and to get up in the morning. The best way to motivate ourselves to make things happen is through goal-setting, so the first part of this chapter looks at this process.

Like Jim, we can learn a great deal about motivation from other people: either directly from the advice of those we admire or trust, or from observing them in action. Therefore, the second part of this chapter looks at how best we can learn from others.

Outer and Inner Motivation

What about those times, though, when it feels very difficult to get motivated? Here it's helpful to think of two types of motivation. The first type consists of 'outer' motivation – goals, rewards and learning that bring us public recognition. The second type is 'inner' motivation – needs and drives that give us personal, inner satisfaction. Identifying these inner needs is a further step to self-knowledge and building confidence, because then we can make sure we choose the right goals; rather than blindly accepting goals that others set for us. We often get in a rut and feel demoralised when we haven't matched our 'inner' needs to 'outer' targets:

Joanna was a sales director for an up-market hotel chain. 'I worked long hours, and earned a very high salary made up largely of commission. The company was my life and a lot of the work was glamorous and exciting. I had little time for a social life outside of work and my friends got used to me cancelling arrangements at short notice. It took a hard knock for me to realise that I was living my life largely for other people's profit. The knock came during my annual appraisal. I had a new boss, and I wasn't sure about his attitude towards me. The appraisal was appalling – although my financial targets had all been achieved and in some instances, surpassed – he criticised my appearance and even my perfume. I knew this was sexist and unfounded – I've always enjoyed expressing what my friends would call "discreet good taste". I was taken aback and upset.

'It set me wondering about my future. I had just started seeing Richard, and I was getting increasingly fond of him, though my hectic schedule meant our time together was rationed. I thought about what I got out of my job. The excitement and social aspects were important, as was the sense of achievement, but I didn't think I was particularly security-conscious, or that predictability of employment mattered. I decided to hand in my notice, and to become a self-employed consultant in the hotel business. While the first few months were tight financially, and I had to work extremely hard, after a year and a half my earnings were up to their previous level, and I was working much shorter hours. Also, I had moved in with Richard.

'Some people have said that I should have taken my ex-boss to an industrial tribunal. But while I agreed with the principle, at that time I couldn't face the hassle. I suddenly realised that I needed different things from those the job was giving me, and I'm really glad I escaped when I did. Taking that decision really boosted my confidence.'

In the final part of this chapter, we look at how meeting *your* needs and matching them to your goals can boost your confidence.

Going for Goals

Goal setting is as useful for motivating other people, as it is for motivating yourself. And the idea has won academic as well as popular approval: '90 per cent of all goal-setting studies showed a beneficial effect of goal-setting on performance' (Edwin Locke, co-author of *A Theory of Goal Setting and Task Performance*).

Why do goals work so well? Because they help us to structure our lives, shape our working hours, and provide us with direction and purpose. With goals, we can exert choice over what we do, and how we do it. And goal-setting can help us, whatever stage of life we're at. In the USA, research with the elderly has shown that when given more opportunity to control and make choices in their lives, the mental and physical abilities improve considerably.

Allowing for change

But goal-setting is not just a question of deciding on a goal, and going for it, regardless of changing circumstances. For the process to be effective, we have to allow for the fact that the world is a dynamic, constantly changing place.

Let's say, for instance, that you have given yourself a goal of promotion, even of getting your boss's job. You are aiming to do this in two years. During the two years however, your company changes dramatically. The department you're in has much less importance because the service you offer the public has become less significant to the company's output. As far as you can see, this lessening of importance is likely to continue. In addition, the whole company changes emphasis. Whereas your strengths are in marketing, where the company has traditionally been strong, the company now decides to place much more emphasis on research and financial control. There is a definite shift in how important marketing people are to the company.

With all this going on, you would be wise to revise your original goal, rather than sticking to it doggedly. As an ambitious person, you might decide you could progress much more effectively elsewhere. If you have become over-attached to your original goal, you could end up being frustrated in your long-term career goals.

This illustrates a crucial theme about goal-setting: *We need to constantly gather information as we proceed to our goals: about ourselves, other people and the environment. We learn and develop as we move towards our goals.* If we become too blinkered about our goals we can easily overlook other opportunities that present themselves.

Mini-goals en route

Practically then, it makes sense to have mini-goals, en route to your main ones, where you can review progress and assess new information and feedback. Perhaps you've got a main goal of building confidence in social situations. You could chart the social events that you attend over a year, as your mini-goals. As you try out new skills, note in a diary what went well, and where there is scope for improvement. (To progress, *always* start with your ovation and then move on to the director's notes.)

Often, too, it can be helpful to see your main goal as at the centre of a circle, or like confidence, at the centre of map, which can be reached by several routes. This helps you to find alternative routes when faced with obstacles. For example, you may try to put new social skills into practice at work, as a route to building confidence in social situations. You have a couple of false starts, where your colleagues make 'helpful' comments such as 'Good God, what's got into you, today?' and, 'Have you been drinking?' Rather than giving up altogether, you could take another route and put your new social skills into practice with friends, in your leisure time. Once you feel that route is working, then you could return to the tougher route of using the skills at work, with your cynical colleagues.

Be specific

It is helpful to be *as specific as possible* in setting goals, as this increases the likelihood of effectiveness in reaching them. A goal like: 'I'm going to get my sales figures up by 15 per cent by the end of year', will be much more effective than: 'I'm going to do my best.' And, 'I'm determined this project will be used as a precedent for all other work in this area', will be more powerful than: 'I'm determined this project will be excellent.' Describe your goal fully, so you know exactly where you are going. Writing down this description, or even drawing in detail how you see your goal will be helpful. It is also helpful to fix a deadline and to plot time steps en route to your goal, where you can review progress and, if necessary, change direction. When your goal is a big one, to avoid feeling overwhelmed by your challenge, it is essential to break your progress down into manageable chunks.

When you choose your goals, it's useful also to think about whether your beliefs and priorities support your choices. In Chapter Two, I talked about the rogue rules which we use to sabotage and prevent us getting what we want. If you choose goals that put very heavy demands on these rogue rules then you may find yourself facing an uphill struggle to achieve them. For instance, if you've got a strong, 'I must always put other people before myself' rule, then deciding to go for a goal of heading up a business empire could be unwise.

Consider priorities

In a similar way, it is useful to consider your priorities, or constructs, which I describe at the beginning of Chapter Three. If, for example, you have as a priority: 'Relationships are very important', then setting yourself a goal of single-handedly sailing around the world, or writing a two-hundred-thousand-word opus, might be unrealistic and cause you more sorrow than satisfaction. It is also worth considering whether your goals and the roles you play are compatible, or whether you can reduce some of the roles you play in order to achieve your goals. You might be stretching yourself if you plan a wide range of goals, such as being a top executive, an ideal wife or husband, a perfect parent, mastering Arabic fluently, oh and not forgetting, attaining a thorough understanding of quantum physics . . .

Having said all that, we do perform better when our goals are difficult, because we put more effort into achieving them. And the more confident we feel, the higher we can set them. This is worth thinking about if we want to motivate others: set realistically achievable goals for the less confident, and quite difficult goals for those people who believe they can do it. Other people will also be more committed if they participate in setting their goals. Ask them whether they think the goals are worth while and what means they will use to achieve them. Find out their realistic expectations of achievement. If you have to set goals for other people without their having a say, then giving them good reasons for the goals can be equally effective. These points are highly relevant to managing people.

CONFIDENCE TRICK: Checklist for Goal-Setting

When you're setting a goal for yourself, or for somebody else, it's worth taking the time to clarify exactly what is involved. That way, you are much more likely to achieve your goal. Ask yourself the following questions:

- Is the goal as specific as it can be?

- What rewards will achieving this goal bring?

- Do I really value these rewards?

- When will the goal be achieved by?

- Can it be broken down into mini-goals?

- How will I know whether the mini-goals and main goal have been achieved?

- From where, and from whom, will this feedback come?

- Who can help?

- What resources do I have that would be of help?

- What lessons have I learnt from goals I've achieved in the past?

Writing down the answers can be very helpful. Research suggests that people are much more likely to achieve their goals when they have committed them to paper, than otherwise. Go for it!

Learning From Other People

In Chapter Three, I described how one of the fundamental ways in which we make sense of the world is through comparing and contrasting – looking for similarities and differences.

If we are ambitious and keen to better ourselves, comparing ourselves with others can leave us feeling frustrated, jealous and lacking in confidence. Other people seem to have had so much more luck, natural advantages or friends in high places, than we have. Now it is a myth that we are all born equal; some people are undoubtedly privileged from the cradle. But when we compare ourselves unfavourably with others, we often do it illogically. We look at 'what' the person is, or has, rather than 'how' they got there. We focus on results, rather than process. Carol freely admits that:

'I used to be quietly jealous of a colleague of mine, Jan. She seemed to have everything: ability, charm, considerateness. She was popular and attractive. She was also extremely well-organised and neatly presented. In contrast, I felt a disorganised mess. Then one weekend we had to go away on company business to a country-house hotel in gorgeous surroundings. We had quite a bit of free time, and I was looking forward to using the spa facilities and relaxing in the lounge with a good book. I thought Jan would do the same.

'But she would have none of it. She rushed around all weekend, organising herself – preparing papers for the following week (unnecessarily), getting her clothes ironed and sticking to her schedule of "organise, organise, organise". When I suggested doing anything spontaneous, she looked appalled.

'I suddenly saw that the "process" of being Jan was no fun at all, even though I admired the end result. I saw that what I did to be "me" was fun and that I enjoyed life a lot more than she did.'

When we resent other people their success, we need rather to ask ourselves: 'How have they got there? What have they done?' Then we get useful information for ourselves. We will see that getting a seat on the board involves mixing with the right people, as well as performing well; that writing a bestseller involves much tenacity, hard work and resilience, as well as talent. We need to look at our role models and ask ourselves: 'What did they do to get here?' and, 'Can I do something similar?' Simply envying them the *results* of their success is futile.

Social psychology experiments have shown that when we judge other people's achievements purely on results, we judge them significantly higher than when we judge them based on process. So if you were to rate the achievements of people you admire, then think about *how* these achievements were reached, and break the process down into steps, and again rate the people, your marks would be lower. This is because, to some extent, we inevitably rank other people's achievements from where we see *ourselves*.

And of course, we are more likely to recognise the steps that *we* can take, when we look at others' achievements in terms of process, rather than result.

Recognising and Satisfying Needs

Goal-setting explains *how* we motivate ourselves. To identify *what* motivates us, we must think about our needs, because when we know what they are, we can use goal-setting to satisfy them – and build confidence and a sense of fulfilment through doing this.

Many different theories have been developed in attempts to explain needs that people might share. Clayton Alderfer's research at Yale University in the 1970s developed what he called the Existence-Relatedness-Growth theory – which evidence supports. In essence, he said that we have:

Existence needs   What we need to survive and to be safe – food, drink, sex, money and a safe environment.

Relatedness needs   What we need to feel attached to, and appreciated by, others.

Growth needs   What we need to feel self-esteem and to fulfil our potential.

All these needs could motivate us at once. When we are frustrated in satisfying one set, then we tend to focus on another. So if you're having problems with relationships and not satisfying relatedness needs, then you may choose instead to concentrate on existence needs, perhaps becoming obsessed with money and security.

The Need for Achievement

Other research has concentrated on what needs get satisfied at work. Here again, identifying *your* needs as an individual can help you to feel confident about making the right choices:

George went to film school, where he was a top student, winning awards. He then spent his twenties and early thirties trying to be successful as a film director, and had some moderate success – but not on the scale that he wanted. He felt extremely frustrated and his confidence suffered. He felt driven, but could achieve little in his chosen sphere. He got more and more disillusioned.

Eventually, George decided to take a couple of months off to review his life. He knew that if he wanted to change direction he would be better off doing it sooner, rather than later. He also realised that he needed to be successful more than he needed to be a film director. Achievement was actually more important to him than what he did. He applied for a job with an advertising agency, as a commercial director, and his subsequent rise to success was meteoric. Once more he was winning awards. Ten years later, George is being offered feature films to direct. So, in recognising his main need – for achievement – he also empowered himself to meet a secondary – but still important need, to direct films.

Do you:

- Set yourself realistic goals?

- Take personal responsibility for much that happens?

- Take initiatives to find new ways of achieving your goals?

- Thrive on new challenges and the unpredictable?

- Get bored easily?

The more 'yes' answers you gave to the above questions, the higher your need for achievement. People who have a high need for achievement are much concerned with improvement, and they are attracted to situations where they see scope for this. You are unlikely to work hard where you see the challenge as too difficult or too easy. Although money and recognition as tangible proof of achievement may please you, you are not strongly motivated by these goals. What does spur you on is responsibility for results and feedback about these results.

The higher your need for achievement, the greater your entrepreneurial spirit. You will have a relentlessness about you that others might find daunting, but which thrives on new challenges. You need to guard against 'peaking early' in your career, where you achieve success early on and then, lacking new goals, become demotivated. Seek to create fresh outlets for your entrepreneurial spirit, in and out of work.

The psychologist David McClelland has shown that people can be trained to increase their need for achievement, which is useful for anyone running an organisation where employees are expected to be entrepreneurial. Effective training involves utilising stories, picture and games to encourage people to think and talk in terms of achievement all day long. Participants will describe their future business plans in terms of milestones for different types of achievement, for instance. They are also encouraged to model their behaviour on that of successful entrepreneurs.

If you don't feel you've a particularly strong need for achievement, worry not. Though this need certainly affected the mood of the 1980s, many people are now valuing a more balanced approach to life, and realising that other needs are also important. Hugh, for instance, re-evaluated his life after his father's death:

'In the mid eighties, I worked in a merchant bank in the city. I was terribly caught up in the Rolex/Porsche/buckets of champagne after work lifestyle. The pace was so frantic I never had time to question what I did, though in retrospect, I realise that I felt anxious quite a lot of the time. Then, my father died. I was very badly affected by his death; my confidence and bravado dissolved. My father had been a very active member of his community and heavily involved in public life. After some soul-searching, I realised that I wanted to contribute more in the way that he did. I took my financial skills and got a very good managerial job in the NHS, which is probably more demanding than my previous one – but also, for me, much more rewarding.'

The Need for Power

This need differs from the need for achievement in that it is to do with gaining recognition and gaining success through your impact on other people. People with a high need for power are good at mobilising others; whereas someone with a high need for achievement may be much more self-centred.

Do you:

- Want to make an impact on people?

- Enjoy being assertive and influencing others?

- Feel reputation and status are important?

- Like making things happen through people?

- Enjoy associating with powerful people?

Again, the more 'yes' answers you gave for these questions, the stronger your need for power.

We can express the need for power in different ways: our hunger for it may cause us to associate with and follow very powerful people, or it may cause us to try and dominate others. How much inhibition, that is, how much self-control we exert on our behaviour will affect how we seek power. David McClelland, the American psychologist who pioneered research into these needs says, for instance, that men who have a strong need for power but a low degree of inhibition will 'tend to think in terms of personally dominating others. They drink too much. They are Don Juans trying to seduce as many women as possible. They lie, trick and deceive. They are socially irresponsible. In short, they have some of the characteristics of the image of Satan.' I'm sure many of us can all think of someone we know like that – and now we know what motivates his (or, with a few essential adjustments to that description, her) behaviour.

On the other hand, people with a high need for power who exert self-control over their behaviour, are socially responsible good citizens. They will want to exercise their power on behalf of others. If they are not over-concerned with how much people like them, they make very good managers. Also, because they are driven to influence others, they may rise higher up the corporate ladder than people with a high need for achievement.

When we talk about power, we are talking about a resource that exists in many different forms. We can have power in terms of our title: 'manager', 'chief executive', or 'finance controller'; power in terms of our expertise and access to information; power in terms of how other people aspire to be like us, and will follow us; power in how we are able to discipline and reward other people. Our power base may be very strong, but not very evident. We may operate most effectively through controlling agendas, through 'who we know', through favours granted and returned. And, of course, confidence will help us to feel personally powerful.

The Need for Affiliation

Both the need for achievement and the need for power are to do with driving ourselves on to gain things, be it targets or reputation and recognition. However, there is a third need which contrasts markedly with either, in that it is not about driving forwards for gain.

Do you:

- Feel relationships take priority over everything else?

- Enjoy liaising between people?

- Think that social contact is extremely important?

- Enjoy being with people just for the sake of it?

- Value time alone?

Positive relationships with others are essential to our thriving and well-being. All of us who choose to live in society have a *need for affiliation*, that is to be with and identify with others. How strong that need is, will affect what we are motivated to do. The more 'yes' answers you gave to the above questions, the stronger your need for affiliation.

With this need, you will be very concerned to create and maintain warm relationships with others. You will also tolerate and value time alone. You will work well in jobs which involve liaison with others, such as a personnel role, for instance, involving negotiation between staff and management, and where relationship factors are most important. However, people with an over-strong need for affiliation act to avoid conflict. They can worry too much about being rejected. They may make poor managers of people because they avoid being direct. To others, they may appear 'unfair' because they have 'favourites' – they work too hard in an effort to get people who don't seem to like them, to do so.

Understanding Motivation

We can learn about our own, and other people's motivation from what is said in conversation. If a person's speech is full of ideas about success, failure, effectiveness and results, then they indicate a strong need for achievement. If they talk about reputation, recognition and influence, and have an impressive title or are very well groomed from head to foot, then they will have a strong need for power. When their concerns are more about relationships and emotions, then a strong need for affiliation may be operating.

Confidence particularly comes from knowing what needs most motivate *you*. None of these needs are exclusive, you could be quite high in a need for power and a need for affiliation, for instance. As we might expect, however, political leaders tend to have a high need for power, while top entrepreneurs tend to have a high need for achievement. The caring professions are likely to have a higher number of people with a strong need for affiliation.

CONFIDENCE TRICK: Needs and Goals

To gain confidence from a sense of self-fulfilment, it can be useful to take an overview of your life, and the extent to which your needs are being met. Where they are not being met, you can then set yourself goals to rectify this.

- Having just read the description of our various needs – for achievement, power and affiliation, you should certainly have a clearer idea of what needs motivate you, much of the time. Look at your life in terms of your work, your leisure time and your family life. Ask yourself to what extent your most pressing needs are met in these three situations. Would you like, for instance, to achieve more at work, to feel more powerful in your leisure time, or to form closer relationships with your family? Or would you like your family to achieve more, to be materially more successful? Perhaps you'd like to form closer relationships with friends in your leisure time, or you would like more influence at work?

- After reviewing areas of your life in terms of how your needs are being met, are there any new goals you would like to set yourself? Sometimes, it can be healthier to have several (a realistic number) of goals you wish to achieve, rather than obsessively pursuing one goal in one area of your life.

Maintaining Motivation

Finally, there are two key points to remember about maintaining motivation, in ourselves, and others. The first is that it's crucial to believe that we will be effective in the challenge we are taking on. Now no-one feels completely effective all the time, so sometimes it's useful to boost ourselves with an 'effectiveness' inventory – a list of lots of things we've done that have made us feel effective. This can act as a mental reminder, as a list we can use in self-talk, or you may find it helpful and confirming to write your list down.

The second point is that we are motivated by rewards that *we* value, *as individuals.* So while money in itself may not motivate you, what it represents in terms of being able to buy you some freedom, or quality of life, or activities and objects that make you happy, will. When we are lacking in motivation, it is always worth checking whether the rewards we are expecting still motivate us. Our values change in life.

Now we are ready to move on to Part Two, in which we look at how Speaking with Confidence can bring us further rewards.

Part Two

Speaking
WITH
Confidence

6 *Sounding Confident*

CONFIDENCE KEY: Sounding relaxed and confident, voice projection, using pitch and clarity to convey credibility and authority

I'VE chosen to start this section on how to communicate with confidence by talking about *how* we use our voices. *What* we say is, of course, very important, but if the tone of our individual voice sounds hesitant, or tense, then we won't convey confidence to others. Many people fail to realise just how flexible the human voice can be, and the extent to which we can control and change the way we sound. Whenever we talk to someone our tone of voice is giving something away, and research shows that if others are in any doubt about our message, they will judge our credibility by how we sound and look.

Accent on Improvement

As we can't *see* our voices working, how they function remains a mystery to many of us. And perhaps because there is still a great deal of snobbery, and inverted snobbery, towards accents in Britain, many people still think that any sort of voice development must mean elocution. Years ago, elocution teachers used to encourage their students to speak with what was either called a Standard English accent or Received Pronunciation. Broadly speaking, this meant English as it was spoken by the majority of people who lived in the Home Counties of England. So people with regional accents, would often strangle the tone of their voices, in an effort to produce an impeccable Standard English accent. Ironically, in trying to speak with the 'correct' accent they would make their voices sound tense, clipped and high-pitched. In films of the 1940s and 50s, for example *Brief Encounter*, you can hear some of the actors and actresses speaking in this rather constipated fashion.

Nowadays, according to the newspapers, Standard English takes the form of what has been called 'estuary English', referring to the area around the Thames Estuary. This describes the London/Essexish accent of people such as Jonathan Ross, the TV presenter. And voice teachers, in the main, no longer train people to strangle their speech. Rather, many hold the view that a well-produced voice is about freeing tension, and encouraging people to make the most of their natural potential. An accent, unless it makes it difficult for others to understand what you are saying – and I will discuss this at the end of this chapter – is not regarded as a disadvantage. As Lenny Henry, Claire Short, Enoch Powell and Jasper Carrott prove, even if you come from the Midlands, with what has been described as the least popular English accent, this need not be a drawback. Indeed, some celebrities capitalise upon their distinctive accents, their readily identifiable sound guaranteeing them column inches. Different regional accents make for a rich symphony of interesting sounds within the British Isles.

Body Talk

The way we speak is affected by our bodies and how we use them. When we feel physically under par, our voices may sound weak and wobbly, too, Psychological factors also play an important part. Terrified of making a presentation perhaps, we may find that our voice seems to get 'stuck' in our throats. Worried about knowing very few people at a party, we may barely manage to mumble introductions.

Many of us, directly or indirectly, are given messages about our voices as we grow up. Perhaps we were brought up as 'nice' little girls, who never spoke loudly. Hardly surprising, then, that as adults we find it difficult to chip in at meetings. As little boys, perhaps we were brought up to shout and to dominate loudly. Hardly surprising again, that we expect everyone to listen to us, and boom out at meetings, ignoring other people's contributions.

Our voices are also affected by how sensitive we are to our own behaviour and that of other people, and how much we wish to be accepted or how much we wish to stand apart. Some of us can't help but pick up on aspects of other people's voices; if they talk loudly we follow; in the company of Americans we find a slight transatlantic drawl creeping into our speech. Or we may have more of a 'you take me as you hear me' attitude, our voices remaining individually distinctive with little adaptation, whoever we are with.

Peer group pressure matters a lot though. Listen to gangs of teenagers speaking, and you will hear what I mean. They will all tend to drawl, for example, if that is the current trend.

Where we live, also has an influence. Living and working in a heavily polluted city, it is quite likely that the pace at which we speak will reflect the pace of life and that we may sound nasal, because of the poor quality of the air that we breathe.

How we speak will affect the confidence we convey to strangers, to people on the phone, to interviewers, to bank managers, to anyone we may be attempting to influence. Although your voice will inevitably be affected by who taught you to speak, and who you copied, each of us has a unique speaking voice. We can all learn to use this instrument to convey confidence.

Straight Talking

Good posture, as well as helping you to create a good impression visually, is of great benefit to a strong voice. Slump and at the same time try to speak loudly, and you will feel and hear what I mean. Your ribs will feel compressed. You won't be able to get enough breath out to create a big sound, and you will lack energy.

Good posture is about comfortable alignment of the body, with the sense that the body is suspended from a string holding you up from the crown of your head. Your neck and shoulders should be relaxed, your chest neither too concave or too convex, your stomach neither too tightly clenched in (it is exercises like sit ups, rather than tension that solve the flab problem, so I've been told) nor too pushed out, so that your lower back caves in. Your knees should be relaxed, not tight as though you are standing to attention, and your weight should be distributed slightly more towards the balls of your feet, than your heels.

Many forms of exercise can help to improve posture, as can alternative therapies such as Yoga and, above all, the Alexander technique, which can undo years of poor postural habits. See the book list for further details.

A Sigh of Release

In situations where our confidence plummets, we may find our breathing pattern changes. Breath produces sound: as the breath travels up into the throat it strikes the vocal cords in the larynx and sound is produced. So the wobbly voice quality that many of us experience when we are nervous, and which gives the speech a hollow sound, is caused by the way breath is leaving our body.

Our breathing changes because, when we are nervous, we experience a 'fight or flight' response. Physically, we start to prepare to escape or attack, even though the likelihood of us actually needing to carry out one of these actions is slim. We put too much effort into getting breath into our bodies and we start to over-breathe. If we continue to do this for any length of time, then we risk hyperventilation – so, if your breathing changes when you get nervous, it's worth learning some breath control. How we breathe also affects our use of pace and pause, our ability to project our voices, and occasionally, how we use pitch.

To feel how little effort you need to breathe to create sound, just let the breath drop down into your lungs, as you breathe in. Place a hand on your stomach and you should feel it push out gently as the breath drops into your body. As you breathe out, sigh gently. This is how easy it is to produce sound. Taking a few easy sighs can help to relax our breathing.

CONFIDENCE TRICK: Taking a Breather

Good breath control can really help you to sound and feel confident.

- Before going into any difficult situation, check that your posture is good. Stand tall, and check that your neck is relaxed by nodding your head gently; give your shoulders a gentle roll. Sigh a few times to check that you are breathing easily. As you walk into the room, or up to the stage, or before you start to speak, take a few easy breaths, reminding yourself to breathe out slowly as you do so. As you breathe in, remind yourself that your breath is just dropping into your body. There should be no short intakes of breath, resulting in a gasping sound, and no obvious effort in your chest and shoulders.

- Get into the habit of taking slightly more time to answer the phone or to reply to question, being aware that it will be well spent in taking your breath in ready to speak. A couple of seconds more before you respond is not going to adversely affect your efficiency. On the contrary, you will sound much more self-possessed.

Pacing Speech

Many of us don't realise that the basic reason why we pause when we speak, is because we need to take in air. The pace at which we speak is decided by our need for pauses as well as the rate at which words tumble out of our mouths. Fast speakers can be very compelling, conveying urgency and commitment. And although the average rate of speaking is about a hundred and thirty words a minute, as listeners we can receive messages at about three times that rate, so we are perfectly capable of comprehending fast speakers. However, you will know yourself that if you have been on the receiving end of someone who talks extremely quickly, it can become relentless. There is no sense that anyone else can get a word in, and the sensation is akin to that of being on the auditory receiving end of a firing range.

Why do we tend to gabble? Often, because our minds are working very quickly, but also because we may give ourselves messages such as 'I mustn't take up other people's airtime', or 'I don't want to risk boring people', or 'If I blurt it all out quickly, then I can get it over very quickly'. All of these messages show a strong flight response. In not giving ourselves time to pause, we can create poor breathing patterns, sound as though we are not considering our listeners' responses, and suggest to others that we are compromising our self possession – we dare not control time at all. The other unfortunate side effect can be that, as speakers, we find our mouths so fully engaged that they leave our brains behind. We end up thinking, 'Oh no, did I really say that!'

So, if you do tend to gabble when your confidence is low, I recommend that you consciously work on taking longer pauses and being aware that you take breath in during these pauses. If you enjoy your momentum when you start to speak, you can still keep a rapid rate of delivery. You will find, too, that if you give yourself fairly generous pause time, you will need to take fewer pauses. As you are taking in more breath, you will be able to speak for longer periods, before coming up for more air. If you are aware that you 'um' and 'er' a great deal, when you get nervous, be aware that you are taking up valuable pause time with these sounds. Resolve rather to make the most of your pauses: to recharge physically, to recharge mentally, and to check and respond to the reactions of your listeners.

CONFIDENCE TRICK: Pause Please

- When chatting to friends and colleagues, talking on the phone, or in meetings, listen to how you use pauses as you speak. If you would like to improve your use of pauses, work with a tape recorder. Imagine you are talking to someone and trying to convince them of something you are enthusiastic or passionate about. Record yourself speaking for about three minutes, then play it back.

- Listen to your pauses. Are your breaths clearly audible, indicating that you are snatching at intakes too quickly? Are you taking up your pause time with too many 'ums' or 'ers'? A few of these are natural, they are simply the sounds of us thinking aloud. But too many of them will sound like a nervous mannerism.

- Then re-record yourself, conveying the same sentiments, using roughly the same words, but consciously thinking that you are pausing for breath every time you breathe. Really labour these pauses if necessary. Then play it back. Is it too slow? Is the quality of your voice sounding richer for having better breath control? Keep working with the tape recorder, until you find a pace that you feel comfortable with, and which makes you feel you are giving yourself – and your potential listeners – good value from your pauses.

- In interviews and presentations, take time to pause, breathe and think before you answer questions. At the outset of presentations especially, as we ease our audience in to what we are going to talk about, we can often afford to pause for longer than we think. This is because, at the outset – if we are not known to our audience – they are getting used to how we look and sound. They do not really pay great attention to what we are saying until we are some way into the presentation.

Speaking Up

Richard is an accountant in a pharmaceuticals company. He is well-liked at work, but very quietly spoken. At meetings, people are constantly asking him to speak up. He finds it very difficult to do so. 'I've always spoken quietly, and I come from a family of quiet, bookish people. But I've started to realise that people associate volume with confidence, and when I'm talking about the company's reports it's important that I do so with conviction and authority. Not being heard, and being asked to speak up detracts from these qualities.'

After quite intensive training, Richard has learnt to speak louder. We *do* tend to associate volume with confidence, though this is an irrational association. And because we hear our own voices through bone conduction in our heads, we do not experience our own volume levels as other people do. Speaking reasonably loudly is attention-getting. It's saying, 'I matter and what I say deserves to be heard.'

CONFIDENCE TRICK: Getting Heard

To project our voices effectively, we need to check that we are taking in an adequate supply of breath (see above) and that we are not constricting our voices in the throat, or through the speech organs: the tongue, teeth, lips and jaw. Throat construction will often result in a strident quality in our voices.

- To ease this tension, we need to learn to relax the neck and throat (again see above) and to practice projecting our voices by throwing 'hoe' or 'ha' sounds to different distances. It will help if you can project to a voluntary audience of one who can move progressively further away and let you know whether you are still clearly audible.

- Yawning is a good way of relaxing the throat, so you might want to have a good yawn if you feel your throat tensing up, before you get up to speak. But don't do this just before you start a presentation to the board . . .

- Though it sounds a contradiction, the best way to project the voice effectively, is to experiment with the stage whisper. This is produced by plenty of breath, and exaggerated articulation, really moving the muscles in the face, so that the words are very deliberately enunciated. Then up the volume a notch or two, and continue to work the muscles as though you are confiding in someone. This gives your speaking voice a very personal intimate quality. This technique is often used by people who are described as 'charismatic'. Practise in front of a mirror until you get just the right degree of muscle movement, so that you feel comfortable and don't look as though you are over-enunciating.

Speakers who tend to under-project their voices need to check also that they are making sufficient eye contact, to see whether their message is being received by their audience. If people look uncomprehending, then you need to speak up. If you know you have a tendency to be too quiet, then, when it matters, ask if everyone present can hear you. This is an insurance policy against the wise-guy who will be only too keen to shout, 'Can't hear you, darling', or 'Come again, mate'. Bear in mind too, that slightly varying the volume of delivery is crucial to being thought of as confident, and of keeping people listening as you speak.

Pitch and Resonance

Two other aspects of voice production help to determine how we sound when we speak. They are our use of pitch and of resonance.

Pitch describes the 'key' or general note of voice we use when we speak. Women generally, with slightly shorter vocal cords, have higher pitched voices than men. Interestingly, very recent research from Flinders University in Australia has shown that the pitch of women's voices generally, is getting lower than it was forty or fifty years ago. This suggests perhaps that social conditioning has affected how we speak, with pre-feminist women having been encouraged to speak in a 'feminine' manner, whereas now we are more likely to find a high, girlish voice irritating in a grown woman.

We all have a natural middle note in our voices, around which we go up and down in pitch. Some of us, when we feel nervous can find our pitch rising generally, or find ourselves using lots of pitch rises. Try saying this last phrase as a question, to hear what I mean. Now in situations where you want to put what you're saying as a tentative proposal, or to get a response from others, this use of pitch is entirely appropriate. But if you want to sound confident and definite about what you are saying, then it's much better to use a technique favoured by TV newsreaders. Bring your pitch very definitely down at the end of phrases. Try this last sentence conducting yourself with a finger, which you pull down on the word 'down' and on the word 'phrases'. Make sure that you don't bring the volume down as well, or people will have difficulty in hearing you.

This technique is useful, too, if you are aware that your pitch tends to rise generally, when you get nervous. Using plenty of pitch drops will anchor your sound.

CONFIDENCE TRICK: Pitching It Right

- At interviews, and when you are being asked difficult questions at meetings or in presentations, remember to make the most of pitch drops. You will sound definite and conclusive, and interviewers will have a clear sense of when you have finished your answers.

- On the phone, if you need to be assertive, or to get through to strangers, this technique can again help, so it is well worth practising in private. Try saying, 'I need you to do that', with the pitch rising at the end, and then try it with the pitch dropping. You can do the same with a request like, 'Can I speak to the head of personnel, please?' You will hear that if your pitch rises dramatically, it sounds tentative and lacking in confidence. You're almost saying to the person on the receiving end, 'I know there's a very slim chance of me getting through here . . . but . . .'

In contrast, if you make the request using pitch drops, it almost sounds as though you're saying, 'I expect to get through to this person, and there shouldn't be any problem.'

Resonance is about the use of space in the body, through which the sound travels. When a speaker has a nasal quality, then too much air is being released through the nose. When you have a cold, and your voice sounds strange, it's because air is unable to be released through the nose. Margaret Thatcher substantially changed her resonance balance, by using more space at the top and back of the mouth for the sound to reverberate through. Changing a voice to this extent can sound unnatural, and to avoid this possibility, the speaker needs a huge amount of application and motivation.

Most people can improve their voices quite considerably by working on breathing, projection, pitch – and clarity.

Accent on Clarity

Clear speech is undoubtedly an asset in creating an impression of confidence. Speech is made up of consonants and vowels.

Consonants   t, d, c, g, m, n, p, b, l convey the clarity and logic of the message. If we've got into the habit of being lazy with our muscles when we speak, and not bothering to put much energy into forming the consonants, then we will not sound clear and logical. We'll end up sounding half-hearted and indecisive. And this sound will have a contagious effect on others; they will begin to feel half-hearted and indecisive in their response to us and what we are saying. So it's important to put some energy into working the muscles of the face when we speak. To get an exaggerated version of this, imagine that you are in a Noel Coward play, and try enunciating everything 'terribly, terribly crisply'. You might sound ridiculous, but you will also sound very definitely decisive . . . Now try gradually reducing the degree of exaggeration until you arrive at a clear but natural delivery.

We can tone up the muscles involved in making consonants very quickly. Refer back to the confiding technique described in the voice projection section, and make a conscious effort to enunciate precisely every time you speak on the phone. Quite quickly, you should notice an improvement in how clear and confident you sound when you speak. If you consciously make the most of all the available space you have in your mouth as you speak, then your vowel sounds should improve as well.

Some accents, Cockney for instance, miss out letters. To the snobbish, not appreciating the vitality of this accent, such omissions may sound like sloppy speech. To prevent this response, rather than changing an accent, it may be worth taking slightly longer to form words so that you *do* make all the sounds. Rather than, 'Cu o tea, please', take time to make it, 'A cup of tea, please'.

If you have an accent that other people have difficulty understanding, you need to check the following:

- Am I speaking loudly enough? (Social conditioning especially for Asian women may affect this.)

- Am I speaking clearly enough?

- Am I giving people enough pause time?

If you answer 'yes' to all these questions and you *still* think your accent is acting as a disadvantage, then you might want to visit a voice specialist, to 'clean up' the sounds that are causing you most difficulty.

Larynx Love

As our voices are unique to us, we should enjoy using them and making the most of them. If you are self-conscious and tentative about speaking, then experiment with your voice – sing really loudly in the bath, try out on a tape recorder the techniques described in this chapter, take singing lessons, join a choir or a drama group. Read plays aloud, taking all the different parts and putting on suitable voices.

Voicework can be therapeutic and most beneficial in confidence building. Once we get to enjoy and savour the sound we make, we are much more likely to use it effectively – and confidently – on others.

7 *Talking Business*

JOAN is a bright young manager in the civil service who has to attend lots of meetings:

'Beforehand I always know what I want to say, but when I get in there, I find it very difficult to speak up. I feel very self-conscious when making my points, and sometimes I think I sound aggressive in order to be taken seriously. It's very frustrating because I know that most of my ideas are good. It's just translating them into business talk that's the problem. I'm ambitious and in the civil service there is a high value on being articulate and fluent. I'm both these things with my friends but at work, in meetings, when it really matters, I lose confidence.'

Many of us are not brought up to talk well. Perhaps our families are very reserved and communication is sparse. We may have been told off by teachers for asking too many questions and talking in class, distracting from the lesson and teacher control. We may have had noisy sisters and brothers, with whom it was difficult to get a work in edgeways. In Britain, in particular, and in marked contrast with America, there is a strong cultural value on modesty and self-effacement and we may have been brought up believing that demanding attention for what we want to say, is 'showing off'.

At work, and when we're socialising, however, other people are rarely aware of, or interested in, the conditioning that has made us who we are. What they see and hear is what they get. The ability to talk well, to express what you want to say and to involve other people in your ideas is a valuable skill: one that can benefit your career and your relationships with others. We can use this ability to make and build contacts and business, to exchange ideas and to realise our goals. Confident at making conversation, we can handle many situations – from unexpectedly arriving in the lift with the chief executive, to putting an unpopular idea to a meeting. And the good news is that we can learn talking skills.

Shyness and Self-Consciousness

In Chapter Five, I mentioned how we often compare ourselves to one another in terms of an end effect or outcome, rather than a process, that is, how we get to be as we are. So we see someone who appears to have every area of their life under control: career, relationships and leisure time, and we envy their powers. We appear shambolic in comparison. What we are ignoring though is how this person got to this state. Perhaps they have missed a lot of fun and spontaneity en route, or maybe they organise everyone around them with a ruthless efficiency that is deeply resented. Where our lives appear shambolic, they may be that way because en route to where we are at present, we have seized all sorts of opportunities, lived for today and made a wide circle of friends.

Shyness and self-consciousness is also to do with this type of thinking. We become fixated with the *effect* we are having on other people, rather than what we are doing in the process of communication. So we enter a room full of strangers thinking, 'They're all thinking I'm fat/ stupid/wrongly dressed/poor/nervous.' Were we to think more about what we are *doing*, we would enter the room, thinking 'I'm greeting/ welcoming/researching/charming/engaging with/involving/the other people in this room.'

How do we stop viewing ourselves in terms of effect? Well, the first crucial assumption to change is that other people are all that interested in us. Many psychological studies show that the majority of us, most of the time, are motivated by *self*-interest. Put yourself on the receiving end of a shy person's entrance to a room. Are you that bothered that they blush, or that interested in criticising their clothes/impression/ body size/intelligence/nervous demeanour? Unlikely, unless you're feeling very inadequate yourself and trying to find someone who appears the same. Indeed, unless the situation is confrontational, or one where you are under close scrutiny – such as at a job interview – then at most times, we need to attract and focus people's attention on to us, rather than have to repel a critical examination.

To an extent then, shyness and self-consciousness are forms of self-obsession. We need to focus our attention out and to view ourselves as active participants in a situation rather than as passive targets of criticism. Again, the role of researcher can help. Give yourself several research questions to answer about the situation:

- What type of people are here?

- How many blondes/brunettes/redheads?

- What's the breakdown of the sexes?

- How are people dressed?

- What does their appearance say about them?

Play around with two or three of these questions in your mind, like an endless cassette tape. As well as helping you focus outwards, this will also give you valuable information about the event. Use this researcher role, too, in situations that call for buckets of confidence – as when sitting on a conference platform as a speaker or member of a panel, waiting to be introduced. Looking interested in your audience will prevent you appearing ill-at-ease or affected in your behaviour.

Another good method of focusing outwards is to think in terms of your actions, that is, what you are going to *do* in the situation. On courses, we often see people behaving as though the only way they can be effective is by being physically busy. This is, of course, not true. We are mentally processing our experiences and making sense of them all the time. Standing in front of a group of strangers, just by looking and smiling gently we are inter-acting with them in other ways, too – analysing, reassuring, interesting and maybe encouraging them. So our process of communication is best described by active verbs rather than by using nouns and adjectives, which more usually describe effect or outcome ('I'm being judged an idiot', or 'I'm inadequate', for instance). You can probably add some verbs of your own to the list at the end of the earlier *Shyness and Self-Consciousness* section of this chapter.

CONFIDENCE TRICK: New Action

When you've got into the habit of always being concerned about the *effect* you create, then you need to rehearse different actions at home.

- Practise walking into a room, sitting at the meeting table, and then looking round an imaginary group in a manner that says: 'I'm reassuring you', or 'I'm encouraging you', or 'I'm welcoming you'. Do your body language, facial expression and movement feel as though they are matching your intention, that is, your action? Be aware that there are over a thousand different active verbs in the English language which describe different activities in communication. You have a great many to choose from. Though you may feel as though you are 'acting' when you do this exercise, it is indispensable practice for behaving with self-assurance in real-life situations.

- When you are nervous, use your chosen action as an affirmation. Check that you are breathing slowly and easily, and run your instructions through your mind as you enter the room: 'I'm reassuring people. I'm breathing easily.' Keep repeating these instructions to yourself.

When we're shy and self-conscious, we worry too much about 'looking good'. We feel uniquely isolated and that we cannot connect with other people. We forget that there may well be other people present who also feel ill-at-ease, and that the majority of us get relief from sharing our responses with others. So when you feel self-conscious, let someone know that you're not entirely comfortable. Disclosure is a powerful ice-breaker in conversation, and we often feel better after it. When you go to an event knowing no-one, then find someone else who looks as though they've come alone, and let them know that you feel slightly apprehensive. You could say for instance: 'Do you mind if I join you? This is my first time here and I feel a bit at sea/uncertain what to expect/at a loss.' They will probably be very relieved to disclose similar information back to you. When we let other people know that we are only human, we literally take them into our confidence.

Remember too, that though the majority of us may be motivated by self-interest, we also enjoy getting involved with or helping others. It is gratifying to be needed and then to be able to solve a problem. So where appropriate, ask other people for help. When you don't know anyone at a meeting or presentation, then explain this to someone who looks approachable, and ask them to introduce you to some people. Only sadists will refuse.

Finally, some of us become fixated with our physical responses to shyness and self-consciousness. It's worth remembering that our bodies are changing all the time according to what we are doing. Clammy hands, blushing, or a wobbly voice are not the end of the world, and a warm smile or witty comment can draw attention away from them. Psychologists have tried many different ways to help people with problems like chronic blushing. The most successful method is to play the endless inner tape of questions, as described above. Keep focusing out on to, and researching, other people present: it's the surest way to minimise these self-conscious responses.

Talk Hang Ups

Some of us give ourselves quite specific negative messages about conversation. Here's a selection:

I'd better not say anything in case it causes offence . . .

Anthony is a university lecturer who greatly enjoys talking. But he never used to. When he was a student, he never opened his mouth in seminars, although his mind was full of ideas. He told me he was convinced that the other students would think he was trying to dominate, if he spoke up. He could see there was logically no likelihood of this, as he never ever said anything at all. But the fear prevailed until he became a lecturer in Italy, where his very job title obliged him to speak out, at length, and where the ease with which he managed to talk to students in a foreign language convinced him that he had a right to speak up in English, as well.

When we have a strong fear that people might isolate us, and reject us, we often contribute little to conversation. We can be especially loathe to express our opinions. In consequence, we may appear compliant and weak to others, or even arrogant – in that we seem as though we can't be bothered to say anything. We risk appearing as though we don't really want to get involved in anything.

We need to remember that we can't expect *everyone* to like us. And that a certain amount of conflict of interest is inevitable when more than one human being is involved in something. We need to face up to the glaring truth that, as individuals, we often want different things. And that living and working comfortably together is probably more about negotiation and compromise than anything else.

The other thing to remember is that you are not your opinions. They may represent an aspect of your personality; but if people disagree with your views, that is not the same as them saying that they disagree with your existence. We need to appreciate that it is opinions and conviction that make any form of communication interesting. To get used to expressing our thoughts, we could start by expressing opinions over less important matters – like where we would prefer to go for lunch with our colleagues – and then graduate to bigger subjects – like why we should really have our boss's job . . .

If I cause offence, then I won't risk anyone trying to get too close to me . . .

We will approach talking in a different way if we fear loss of identity and distinctiveness. We could be deliberately offensive and provocative; hoping this will act as a warning beacon to others not to come too close. Or we might be incapable of listening to anyone else, our self-image being so fragile that we cannot even risk considering other people's opinions and contributions. Establishing 'this is who I am' is all that matters.

About six years ago, I was giving a talk to a group of businesswomen in the City. At the end of the talk, as we were having drinks and nibbles, a woman called Louise engaged me in conversation. She told me that very recently she had changed professions; but she was highly opinionated and disagreeable, even angry and bitter. I didn't envy her new colleagues at all.

Four years later, I met Louise again, through a professional cause. She seemed to be a different person. We became good friends, and I asked her whether it was just my perception that she had changed dramatically. 'No,' she said, 'when you first met me, my husband of ten years had just left me. I had made a big decision to move from education into business, and I was desperately uncertain of my identity. I was going around being bolshie and difficult with everyone – because I felt emotionally battered. I tried to appear tough and supremely self-confident – which was the last thing I felt inside. It took me quite a time and a lot of hard work to feel better.' Louise is now content, delightful to be with and she works very successfully, as an outplacement counsellor.

When appearing independent and imposing our identity on others is too important to us, then we prevent ourselves listening to others. This means that we don't hear valuable feedback that could help us match our own perceptions with reality, and so we distance ourselves from the truth. In worrying that other people might want to get close to us, we may be denying the need for close relationships and intimacy that all of us have, when we are psychologically healthy. We are also overlooking the extent to which conversation is about an exchange of information, as much as relationship building.

We can become more adept at talking by considering what makes us distinctive, feeling secure about it, and appreciating distinctiveness in others, as something to be valued, not as a threat. To find out about other people's distinctiveness we need to engage them by asking open questions which require substantial answers, such as: 'How did you enjoy that?' 'What happened then?' and listening attentively. We can also appreciate how much human beings have in common with one another, and look for shared interest and goals in the conversation.

If I start to enjoy talking, I may reveal too much about myself . . .

Brian is an accountant. When he talks, he does so in a stilted fashion. He appears to think very carefully before he speaks, and his speech is over-correct: he says 'one' a lot, rather than 'I', 'you', or 'we'. He says, 'one does not' and 'they cannot', for: 'I don't', and 'they can't'. At meetings, he has noticed that people appear to get irritated or bored when he speaks for any length of time.

When we fear loss of control, we can find it very difficult to talk with spontaneity and lack of inhibition. The censor in our heads will cut what we want to say, before the words are allowed to get out of our mouths. As humour usually involves making spontaneous connection between different aspects of something, we find it difficult to make humorous comments, jokes and witticisms. Our responses are always measured and considered, and other people may find it difficult to relax in our company. We are worried by people who seem overly emotional, enthusiastic and uninhibited in conversation. We become uncomfortable when topics we hadn't planned for come up, and as we can't prepare for it very much, we won't enjoy making small talk.

A preoccupation with control is to do with structuring and ordering events and people so as to avoid chaos, at all cost. As far as possible, we want to insure how things will turn out. We see ourselves as having sole responsibility for being in control. This, of course, is not true. We only have limited control over the behaviour and actions of others. Life is such that unpredictable events will occur.

We also worry that if we reveal our true selves, then other people will discover our weaknesses and exploit them. So we go on our best behaviour and talk in a stilted, slightly artificial way. In fact, while a small minority of people might display the vindictive attitude we fear, the majority of us find spontaneous and open conversation very enjoyable. We need to remember that a lot of conversation is not that important anyway, but to listen attentively to what others say, and respond spontaneously, making comments that connect with their content. Viewing some conversations as opportunities to let other people get to know us better can help. Turn your personal censor off.

If I say that, they'll think I'm stupid . . .

John is the only member of his team of engineers who had a university education; the rest have practical qualifications. Deep down, this eats away at John's confidence. He doesn't like to ask the others for help and goes on about his university days so much that the rest of the team have nicknamed him 'Mortar board' . . .

When we are unsure about our competence, we again edit what we say – this time, in case other people think us stupid, and lacking in information. If something comes up in conversation that we don't know much about, we find it impossible to ask questions and show our ignorance. We might also become over-concerned with airing our knowledge about subjects we *do* know a lot about, correcting other people at every opportunity and supplying irrelevant details.

When we do this, we place too much importance on ability and knowledge as the meaning of who we are. We take ourselves too seriously, which is why we can't risk admitting we don't know something. Other people will sense this, and use humour to bring us down a level, as John's colleagues did. We need to remember that the only way to continue to learn, is by acknowledging what we don't know. We can also usefully rehearse such phrases as: 'I don't know much about that, can you tell me more, please?' After all, if you enjoy airing your areas of expertise, why deny others the same pleasure – particularly when such conversations also help to build and strengthen relationships?

The Exchange Game

When conversation works well, people are involved in constantly exchanging information, opinions, challenges and entertainment with one another. It's like playing bat and ball, one of us gives, the other takes and then throws some words back . . . and so on. The rules of the conversation game are simple and can be quickly learnt.

In conversation, there are only six options open to us. We can:

- State an opinion.
- State a fact.
- Ask a question.
- Talk about ourselves.
- Talk about the other person.
- Talk about the situation.

Most of us choose to be measured by our opinions when we first meet strangers, and these conversational gambits are often obvious: about the weather, the traffic, or the number of people present. This doesn't matter; the purpose of small talk is less about *what* we say than *how* we say it. Small talk allows us to get the flavour of the other person, and to decide whether we would have things in common, whether we would like to get to know him or her better, or whether we might do business together. And the good news for those of us who are conditioned to value modesty and self-effacement, is that often the best conversational-ists spend more time talking about the other person, than themselves. However, they also know when it's appropriate to use some personal disclosure to help the other person relax and open up.

Small talk works to a formula. Someone makes a comment: on the occasion, the news, the people, the food and drink, and then asks a question to involve the other person. For example: 'It's very busy here. Have you been here long?' Now this is hardly sparkling stuff, but it indicates to the other person that we are opening a conversation. We usually move from the general to the more specific: 'How do you feel about the prospect of relocation?'

Open questions get other people talking. Questions like 'What was that like?' or 'How did you think/feel that went?' or requests like 'That sounds interesting, can you tell me more?' We can encourage people to continue talking by showing evidence of interest: nods of the head and mns of encouragement. And also by summarising, as in: 'So you'd finished the project completely by then', or paraphrasing what you think the other person means, 'So you were pretty pleased with yourself.' These are also useful for eliciting confirmation that we have understood a particular point correctly, or having it further clarified.

CONFIDENCE TRICK: Conversation Boosters

- Improve your listening skills, by encouraging your friends and family to talk to you about any problems they may be having. Restrain yourself from offering solutions and advice; just concentrate on summarising and paraphrasing during the conversation. This is a very generous act, to really listen to another person, without taking any power from them by telling them what to do, but rather letting them clarify their own feelings and ideas. And from your point of view, you can't be too good at listening. It's the most valuable skill for learning about what makes other people tick and can often tell you things about yourself, too.

- Pay more attention to news stories (take two newspapers: a broadsheet and a tabloid if you want lots of material) and controversial television programmes, and decide on your views about them. What are your reasons for arriving at these opinions? These news stories can also provide subjects for conversation, during which you will be able to air your views in a considered and individual way.

- Give yourself an overall goal when you get into situations where you might otherwise feel tongue-tied. This purpose should be about you taking an initiative: like meeting three new people, or making someone there feel really good, or finding out some specific information. This takes me back to my teenage years when, on Saturday nights, we all had the goal of 'going home with someone' – though we all pretended otherwise. And oh, the abject sense of failure if we didn't!

Can I say something please?

Even quite confident people can find themselves quaking if they go to a meeting, presentation or social event and realise they know absolutely no-one there. A friendly smile, with a request for help and some disclosure are the best tactics. When everyone is standing around in groups, holding conversation, approach the one that looks most open in terms of grouping. Say 'hello', and that you don't know anyone here, so could you join them?

When we've been brought up to communicate in a polite and considerate fashion, the cut and thrust of business talk can be daunting, especially the need to interrupt. We interrupt to dominate others, but also to show enthusiasm and keenness to get involved. In my experience, women tend to be generally better listeners than men, and have more difficulty in interrupting. We need to learn to speak up clearly and loudly, and if we are ignored, to keep repeating our request to be heard. Humour can help, especially if we know other people present quite well. A self-deprecating comment such as: 'Gosh, I must be really insignificant, the way everyone keeps ignoring me', can stop everyone in their tracks, make them laugh, and give you the floor.

Letting people know how you feel about interrupting, can make you feel more confident about it. For example: 'I feel rude constantly chipping in like this but . . .' Don't shy away from using body language to help your purpose either: waving frantically at a chairperson usually ensures that you get attention.

In meetings, if you tend to be reticent about speaking up, make yourself say something in the first five minutes. Otherwise, it will get increasingly difficult to say anything at all and your internal censor will get more and more critical about your potential contribution. *What* you say for this 'opener' needn't be that profound: you can just ask what time the meeting finishes, whether so and so is coming or request that a window is opened. The important point is to get used to speaking up and hearing your own voice in the meeting, early on, and it establishes your presence so that when you speak again – on a specific matter of importance – you will more readily get attention.

Setting Boundaries

Skilled conversationalists have a knack of controlling conversation in a very subtle way. How? Well, they will often introduce subjects and determine the agenda. They may look puzzled if you introduce a subject that they don't want to talk about, and give a reason for not discussing it: 'That's rather at a tangent', or 'Can we talk about that later', or perhaps use humour to subtly dismiss it: 'Ouch, that subject hurts my ears, can we change it, please?'

Tactical talkers will set the boundaries for the interaction. 'I've got fifteen minutes to discuss this', or 'I need to be at another meeting in half-an-hour'. They will use a diagnosis of how the conversation is going as a controlling device. 'We've got rather away from the main points now.'

Finally, confident conversation is about not trying too hard. Long sentences, with subordinate clause after subordinate clause, and many phrases and additional ideas, joined by 'ands' and 'buts' can be very difficult to follow. This is even more true of the spoken word, than the written one. Rambling thought patterns do not translate well, directly in to speech. So it will help you to sound confident and decisive if you speak in short sentences. Remarkably easy to do.

8 *Asserting Confidence*

CONFIDENCE KEY: Saying no, taking criticism, giving criticism, making requests, handling compliments

---

IN RECENT years, assertiveness training has become very popular. It provides a useful set of skills for confidence building, especially in helping us know *what* to say when we are in situations that challenge our confidence. As some of the best-known books on assertiveness have been written for women, people sometimes think it's a 'woman's thing'. This isn't the case; assertiveness offers skills that are equally useful to men and women. It helps those of us who are clumsy and overbearing in our dealings with others, as well as those of us who are passive and compliant.

Ideally, assertiveness helps you stand up for yourself without causing harm to others. Some courses and books on the subject contain a bill of rights, which includes: 'The right to make mistakes', 'The right to say no without feeling guilty', and 'The right to be listened to and taken seriously'. In real life, this list can have limited application, because while *we* may be aware of it as our bill of rights, other people may not.

Assertiveness puts behaviour into three categories:

- Assertive behaviour, where we get our needs and rights respected while respecting those of other people.

- Aggressive behaviour, where we get our needs and rights met, while ignoring those of other people.

- Submissive behaviour, where we allow other people to get their needs and rights met at the expense of our own.

Submissive behaviour is not good for our health. When we passively allow ourselves to become doormats for others, while suppressing what we want, we become angry and frustrated inside. We put other people before ourselves, expecting that they will return the consideration. When this doesn't happen, we feel that we've been treated unfairly – when of course, the other people haven't asked us for special consideration in the first place. We may have learnt this behaviour from our parents, or been encouraged by them to act accordingly. Any fan of Woody Allen's films will have heard of characters who are labelled as 'passive aggressive': people who choose to act as martyrs and victims, and are secretly angry about it. So they manipulate others in devious ways to get their revenge. Research has suggested links between this type of behaviour and certain illnesses.

In this chapter, I want to look at five types of assertive skills:

- Saying no.
- Taking criticism.
- Giving criticism.
- Making requests.
- Giving and receiving compliments.

No, No chance, No way

Some of us have great difficulty in saying 'no'. Brought up to please, and to be conciliatory we may find it very difficult to refuse other people's requests. We worry that other people will think we don't like them, or that we're uncooperative. As a result, we can find ourselves working late, having too much responsibility, lending people money, drinking too much and having unwanted visitors to stay. We end up feeling exhausted and resentful.

In Chapter Seven, I wrote about the indirect nature of conversation. The rules of politeness often prevent us from being as direct with one another as we would like too. We can find ourselves, then, when a colleague asks whether we mind taking on extra responsibility, or a friend asks whether we mind if she/he borrows our car, responding vaguely: 'Mm, I don't really mind', or 'Oh, all right'. Really, we would rather be saying, 'No'. Some people are so demanding that even if we give a tentative negative like, 'I'm not really sure about that', they will manage not to hear this response. Before we can blink, we find ourselves holding the report we've been lumbered with, or handing over our car keys . . .

Often, because we have a habitual tendency to please others, we acquiesce and go along with what they want, before thinking what we want. We may ignore our intuition, which in a small but significant voice is saying: 'No, no, no!'

Anna works as a computer analyst in a big company. The marketing department there has a strong reputation for employing 'difficult' bullish people, for in-fighting and conflict with other departments. A marketing manager approached Anna, to help install new software and train his personnel in its use. Strictly speaking, this was outside Anna's remit and job description. But she felt enormously flattered, and despite a whiff of intuition telling her she should bide her time, she agreed immediately. She found herself working till midnight some nights, training people who were resistant and resentful. Once the manager had secured her services – for free because she was 'staff' – he showed little appreciation for what she was doing. Next time, Anna says, she'll listen to her intuitive voice.

CONFIDENCE TRICK: Saying 'no'

- Stall your impulse to please people at your own expense, by pausing before you answer requests you have doubt about. Announce an official delay if necessary: 'Can I get back to you on this one please?', 'I need some time to consider this', or 'Let me think about it.'

  This gives you time to think: 'Am I doing this because I really want to?' and 'Are there rewards in this for me?' and 'What are the rewards for the other person?' Often the rewards may be intangible, such as recognition and appreciation from others.

- Practise saying, 'No', loudly and clearly and in different ways so that you get used to hearing yourself saying it. Be strict with yourself about using the actual word 'no', to communicate directly.

- When you're saying 'no' to a request, don't allow yourself to be sidetracked. Avoid giving too many reasons. You can soften your refusal slightly by using phrases like, 'No,

I'd prefer not to', or 'No, I don't want to.' If you're concerned about sounding hard-hearted and uncooperative, then show that you understand the other person's position with a phrase like, 'I can see that you have a problem but...', or 'I'm sorry that you're overworked but...'

- If necessary, keep repeating your 'no' statement, when the other person tries to divert you:
  Ms Pushy: 'Would you mind helping me out on this report, tomorrow?'
  Mr Assertive: 'No, I'd prefer not to.'
  Ms Pushy: 'Why not? You've not got much on at the moment, have you?'
  Mr Assertive: 'I've plenty to get on with. So I'll have to say no.'
  Ms Pushy: 'But I'm snowed under here ... you know, I'd do the same for you ... please, it won't take you long ...'
  Mr Assertive: 'I can see that you're under pressure, and I'm sorry about that. But I'm still going to have to say no.'
  Ms Pushy: 'Oh, all right.'

Remember, it's not the *person* you are rejecting, it's their *request*.

Taking Criticism

Almost all of us have had our confidence dented by harsh criticism. We may have heard messages from our parents: 'Her brother's got all the brains around here', or 'He's terribly shy, bless him', or 'We're all hoping he's a late developer.' We may have been labelled as 'fatty', or 'stupid', or 'tone deaf', or 'bad at figures' by our schoolfriends and teachers. And the effect of these messages may have been so hurtful that we put up barriers against all forms of criticism. Defensively, we shut our ears when people offer us criticism, whether their comments are constructive, or destructive. We may immediately start to justify ourselves and our behaviour, so that the person offering the criticism is attacked back and discouraged from continuing. Our responses are likely to be most defensive when we suspect that the criticism is accurate . . . ouch, it hurts.

In the long term, this is not useful behaviour. In Chapter Five, where I talked about goal-setting, I emphasised the importance of getting feedback – the 'nice' word for criticism. If we are to have an idea of our progress at anything, we have to be open to criticism.

Criticism is information about how we are seen from other people's perspectives. In any situation we go into, especially when our confidence is low, it's useful to think of the situation from two angles. The first, is our subjective perception of what is going on. When confidence plummets, our perceptions may include ideas like, 'Everyone thinks I'm boring', or 'They all think I'm incompetent'. The second angle, is what is really going on, in terms of objective reality. This is a very difficult state to gauge, and our best way of getting close to it, is to receive feedback from other people. If you suspect you're being boring or incompetent, then the only way to test this perception is *through asking others to comment and inviting them to give you constructive criticism – in the form of praise, where merited, and suggestions as to where you have scope for improvement.* Constructive criticism gets us closer in touch with reality, and adds to our store of information. This builds our personal power and confidence.

It's most useful to learn to do this, and it helps us to deal with a psychological tendency we all have, which is called projection. What we often do is give ourselves messages like, 'You're boring', and 'You're incompetent', and project this reaction onto everyone else present. In other words, we decide that everyone else must be thinking the same negative thoughts. Irrationally, we become mind readers who think we know what everyone else is thinking about us. Rationally, this is clearly not so. Projection works positively, as well as negatively. This is why sometimes, we come across people who obviously think they are truly marvellous and that everyone else should think so too. These individuals become extremely perplexed when they get a conflicting reaction from others, suggesting that perhaps they are not so marvellous. On the whole though, this is probably a more useful attitude to have in life, than to be using lots of negative projection.

Even negative criticism has its uses. Parents dump criticism on their children, because that is the way *they* were brought up. When colleagues and friends give us destructive criticism that we suspect is not true, then whatever they are saying tells us about their agendas and concerns.

It will tell us how they compare themselves with us. John is a fairly recently qualified solicitor:

'I have to make presentations with my boss to clients. This is a new skill for me to master, so I'm quite preoccupied with my own performance. My boss has a very casual attitude towards it; he says people make too much fuss about presenting and there's nothing to it. When we're actually doing the presenting though, he quite often takes the opportunity during breaks and at the end, to haul me over the coals for not having pitched it right, and not matching the clients' needs. I've tried hard to do something about it – really thinking about what I'm going to say beforehand, and analysing the clients' needs and expectations.

'Anyway, the other day, we were presenting to clients, and one of them was an old university friend of mine. We went for a drink after the presentation and his comments were a revelation. He thought my boss had been patronising and insensitive to their needs; while my style and content won praise. When I mentioned my boss's frequent criticisms of my performance, his comment was "hardly surprising".'

As negative criticism can be dumped on us when we least expect it, it's sensible to be prepared for it. There are also ways in which we can usefully encourage people to give us positive criticism.

CONFIDENCE TRICK: Positive Criticism

- **Stay physically relaxed when someone criticises you and let your posture remain open. Lean slightly towards the person, rather than backing away from them or taking up an aggressive position. Respond when you're ready, rather than charging in with a retort before you've given yourself time to think.**

- **If you are uncertain what they mean, ask them for further clarification and to be more specific in their descriptions and examples.**

- **If you suspect the criticism is being given unfairly, ask the person why they are making the comments. If you're not sure about how valid the comments are, then ask someone you can trust for an objective opinion about the criticism. In all instances, it is useful to ask your critic for suggestions** as to how you can do things differently. These suggestions can provide you with constructive practical advice. Or, if the critic is unable to suggest alternative behaviour, then perhaps this reveals that they are not motivated by your best interests.

- Ask yourself what mood the other person is in. Are they being reasonable, or are they inventing things?

- Ignore all criticism that starts with, 'We've all been talking and . . .' or 'Everyone has been saying how . . .'. The critic is suffering from delusions of grandeur.

- When you think the criticism is useful, and the person has your best interests at heart, acknowledge that you've received their points by saying, 'Oh, I'll think about that', or 'That's useful to know', or 'Thank you for that'. They will then be encouraged to make further constructive comments in the future, which will be for your benefit.

- Encourage people to give you useful criticism by asking, 'How did you think that went?', 'Was there any room for improvement?' or, 'What did you think worked and what didn't?'

John Cleese, in *Life and How To Survive It* co-written with the psychotherapist Robyn Skinner, says that he found people very reluctant to criticise his performances and films at Video Arts, his training film company. He discovered the best way to get criticism was to phrase his request in a way which encouraged people to make positive suggestions. At the end of a screening, he'd ask: 'If *you* were making this film from scratch, what would you have done differently?' We can adapt this technique to our own situations: 'Were you to have been organising the team at that time, how would you have done it differently?' or, 'If you were making that presentation, how would you have done it in a different way?' or, 'If you were dealing with the situation at that point, would you have handled him in such a manner?'

Giving Criticism: Courage Counts

When we give criticism in a constructive way, we can boost people's confidence. Giving others specific information about what we like and don't like about their behaviour or performance, will help them to be more aware of their strengths and weaknesses. We can even help people to get more in touch with reality, especially if they are being overly self-critical. Through giving positive criticism, we can help others to develop new skills and we can encourage them to change for the better.

So giving criticism to help others is a generous act; it is also a courageous one. Yet many of us shy away from doing it. When we are hyper-sensitive to receiving criticism ourselves, we suspect that others will react in the same way. We don't want to risk upsetting people or the prospect of them attacking us back. And we need a good measure of self-esteem to feel able to give others criticism. In effect we are saying: 'My opinion is worth hearing and can be valuable to you.'

Susan is a sales rep for a cosmetic company: 'I always find it very difficult to criticise people who do the same job as I do, in my team. But the other day I was out on a visit with Jo, and was really shocked by how she was talking to customers. I knew that if our team manager heard her, she would be appalled. It was important, I thought, to get in fairly quickly. I made myself as relaxed and easy in my manner as I possibly could and, over a cup of coffee, I explained that she risked upsetting customers and losing business in behaving like that. It turned out that she had boyfriend troubles which were on her mind, and that she had had no idea that she was allowing this stress to adversely influence her treatment of customers. She thanked me for being direct and caring enough about her, to tell her. We then talked about what she could do differently.'

When we don't give enough thought to the value of criticism, then we can end up passively putting up with poor standards of work, difficult behaviour from colleagues, friends and family and generally unfair treatment. Or we may voice all our criticism as destructive nagging and blaming, which only makes relationships worse. We can get caught in a vicious cycle of hurting the other person, which in turn, makes us feel worse about ourselves. All sounds very gloomy? Not when you have a few confidence tricks up your sleeve . . .

CONFIDENCE TRICK: Constructive Criticism

- Choose the place and the timing carefully. It is unkind to humiliate people by criticising them in front of others. However, it is best to criticise behaviour fairly soon after it has occurred.

- Test the person's reaction by opening with a question: 'How did you think you spoke at that meeting yesterday?' In some cases, you may not need to make your points, the person will be aware of them already.

- Give people a balanced picture, by recognising their strengths first, and psychologically 'stroking' them: 'Your powers of persuasion are wonderful but . . .', 'You're a really valuable member of the team but . . .'

- Be as specific as you can be about what you are criticising. Use verbs as much as possible, rather than nouns and adjectives. For example, when you tell someone that they were 'wandering off the point' they can choose to do something different. When we use descriptive words and labels, such as: 'You were vague', or 'You're a thinker not a talker', then it becomes much more difficult to understand what should change. Check that the person understands *what* you are criticising.

- Only criticise behaviour that can be changed, and have alternatives ready. Be clear about the positive action the person can take.

- Keep a small number of negative points – the most important ones and those that can readily be addressed. Do not hark back on the past. We can only change the present and the future. The 'And another thing . . .' type of criticism will simply waste your breath.

- Remember you are not God. This criticism you are offering is only your interpretation of events. Check that you don't have any hidden agendas yourself. Are you criticising someone for a weakness that you secretly suspect you share?

Making Requests

As we grow up, many of us are encouraged to put other people's needs before ourselves. We're told to, 'Stop being selfish'. And we're taught how to communicate 'politely', so that we avoid direct statements of what we want and need. Some of us even have difficulty saying the word 'I'. Instead, we'll use an indirect word like 'one'.

This can create all sorts of difficulties in relationships with others. We may expect our boss to know that we want to finish work by a certain time every night in order to see the children. We may assume that our partners can mind read that we want to go to a particular restaurant, when they ask 'Where would you like to go tonight?' and we reply, 'Don't mind especially.' What we really mean, of course, is, 'I want to go to the new Chinese restaurant in the high street.' Then, when our partner suggests getting a pizza delivered . . . well, we sulk.

To be confident, we have to learn to make requests assertively. When people reject these requests, we need to remember it is the *request* they are rejecting, not us *personally*. We have to believe that we have a right to stand up for ourselves and ask for what we want. Otherwise, there is no point in resenting the fact that we never got it. We all have wants and needs that we wish to satisfy. Work and personal relationships work best when these wants and needs are brought out into the open and negotiated upon.

When we do not ask for things clearly, embarrassment and confusion usually reigns:

David wanted to take a long holiday last year, of six weeks, so he could go to America and tour around. Normally in his company, people are allowed to take three weeks holiday at most, at any one time. 'I got myself into a terrible state about asking for this holiday. I put it off, and then when I finally did get round to it and asked my boss if I could discuss something with him, I looked so serious, that he took me off to a private office. When I blurted out my request, he responded by saying, "Oh, is that all you want. I thought you were about to leave, or tell me you had a serious illness." '

CONFIDENCE TRICK: Asking for What we Want

- Be clear and direct in your speech, and work out what you want to say beforehand. Begin with: 'I want', 'I would like', 'I wish', 'I need'. If necessary, keep repeating the chosen phrase, using what's called the broken record technique – especially if you are being sidetracked.

- Anticipate the reaction. If you are worried about how the other person will respond, use phrases like, 'You might be rather surprised at my request', or 'You might think this is very cheeky of me', or 'You may find it inconvenient to grant me this but . . .' Research shows that top business negotiators make great use of these phrases – and they work.

- If you want someone to stop doing something, try the following formula: describe, disclose, predict. For example: 'When you interrupt me all the time in meetings (describing), I feel uncomfortable (disclosing), and if it continues I'll have to mention it to the chair. I want you to stop please.'

- Never underestimate the power of asking others for help. Human beings are often very responsive to this, and flattered to be asked: 'How can you help me with this problem?' often results in much greater compensation than a tirade against the person on the receiving end.

Handling Compliments

Compliments are a form of constructive criticism, and many of us are reluctant to use them. We think we may be regarded as ingratiating or insincere, or that complimenting someone is too personal a form of communication. But giving and receiving compliments with grace breeds confidence. Compliments and praise are also a very effective way of helping people with low self-esteem, as my own experience shows:

A few months ago, I was asked to run a workshop for unemployed people, for a BBC project. The group included two ex-prisoners, and several long-term unemployed. The aim of the workshop was to build the participants' confidence in their communication skills. On day one, my heart sank as I noticed the most difficult member of the group was tattooed with 'Born to lose'. This did not bode well for the rest of two days. He was also hostile, aggressive and very negative. Dispirited at the end of day one, I resolved to work very hard the following day at giving him what Carl Rogers, the psychologist, described as 'unconditional positive regard'. That is, to demonstrate a positive attitude towards him as a person, whatever his behaviour. I also decided that I was going to give him heaps of compliments and positive comments.

At the end of day two, while he was by no means transformed, there was a marked difference in him. He even reluctantly admitted that he had enjoyed the two days greatly and that he felt a lot more confident. Even so, it would take more than a two day workshop to undo decades of thinking that his role in life was that of a victim and an underdog.

CONFIDENCE TRICK: Giving and Receiving Compliments

- Be as specific as you can be. 'That was a great performance', is not nearly as tangible a compliment as, 'You sounded so credible in there, and your argument was watertight.'

- Don't belittle yourself when you compliment others. Give them praise in their own right rather than as a measure of comparison with your inadequacies – real or invented.

- If you're on the receiving end of an ambiguous compliment of the 'Goodness, you look stones lighter' variety – implying perhaps that you looked obese before, speak your mind: 'I'm not quite sure what you mean by that', or 'I'm not certain whether you meant that as a compliment or not.' Keep your tone light and your manner friendly.

- Don't stop compliments by rebutting them. When someone says, 'That's a great outfit', rather than replying with a 'What, this old thing?' which can make the sender feel foolish, accept with grace, 'Thank you very much!'

And thank *you* very much for reading to the end of this chapter so attentively.

9 *Building Relationships*

THE skills in this chapter are quite advanced, so if you are new to self-development, I suggest you make certain that you have understood the more basic ideas in previous chapters, before reading on.

Good relationships are essential for building confidence. They help us in our business and personal lives. When we can communicate clearly with others, express our thoughts and feelings to them directly and make them feel that they can do the same, then the setbacks and problems that life throws up become much easier to handle. Neither too dependent on other people nor too concerned with being separate and different from them, we can achieve a balanced sense of self-fulfilment. In solitude, we do not feel abandoned; in connection, we do not feel overpowered.

This is an ideal situation, which I think is worth aspiring to. In real life, however, while we are striving to fulfil ourselves, we will inevitably have to deal with some people who do not wish to support us in this. As individuals, we often want different things. Many psychologists believe we all have a certain amount of innate aggression, due to the presence of the hormone testosterone. This aggression makes us fight, physically and verbally, with one another; it makes us behave in destructive and disagreeable ways. And, of course, we can use our aggression constructively: debating issues to fruitful resolution, driving through projects, building enterprises, and standing up for human rights and justice. Having confidence is not about denying that we are aggressive and have conflicting interests: rather it is about developing the resources to cope with these facts.

To build relationships with others, we need to be able to influence them and to deal with conflict. Knowing we have these resources can be an immense boost to our confidence. In this chapter, I want to investigate two frameworks that help us do these two things. Both frameworks concern themselves with *how* we speak to one another as well as *what* we say.

Framework 1: Neuro-Linguistic Programming (NLP)

This was developed by two American researchers, Drs Richard Bandler and John Grindler in the early 1970s. They studied people who exemplified 'excellence in performance', and analysed what these people did and said. They then developed their analysis into a set of theories about how we experience the world, and how we communicate our experience. Following on from their research, much has been written about the subject. So if it interests you further, please see the reading list.

At present, NLP enjoys great popularity as a method of training people in influencing skills. As it is about entering the world of another person, it also has widespread application in counselling, selling, presenting, negotiating, leading and managing people. Here are some of what I consider to be some of its more useful and accessible ideas:

Positions please

When we view ourselves communicating, we can see ourselves in one of three positions:

- A **'where I'm at' position**, where we are subjectively concerned with what we want and need.

- A **'where you're at' position**, where we are concerned with what the other person wants and needs.

- A **'detached observer'** position, where we are able to stand back and objectively view, understand and describe what is going on.

Skilled communicators will shift easily from one position to another as appropriate. Let's look at how the three positions manifest themselves in a typical situation where influencing skills are called for:

The Three Positions of Communicators

Jane is talking to a group of businesswomen about her financial services company. She wants to build a relationship with them to sell her services. When she is in the 'where I'm at' position, she talks about her company, its success and her clients. She gives examples and case histories of work they've done. If these are relevant and connect with the particular women in the audience, then Jane's moving into the 'where you're at' position. She will stay in this position while she talks about what she thinks the women's needs are, and when she refers to assumptions she may have made about the women's level of earnings and what's important to them. Jane moves into the 'detached observer' position, when she stops speaking, to organise the seating arrangements for some latecomers. She returns to this position when she sees someone looking puzzled in the front row and says to this woman 'You seem to be looking puzzled. Have I explained that last point clearly enough?' She is back in this position once more, when she says, 'Well this talk has now lasted twenty minutes, which is said to be the maximum time anyone can listen with concentration. Can I take any questions, please?'

In moving round the three positions, Jane will have kept her audience's interest, and shown a breadth of concern and viewpoint which influences others.

Very often, people with communication problems show a lack of awareness of these three positions. The shy person, for instance, who feels unable to make conversation with strangers, and the salesperson who chatters on to the bored customer, are both stuck in the 'where I'm at' position. The person who is incredibly inquisitive and interrogates you about your private life, and the person who relentlessly gives you advice and analyses your problems, is stuck in the 'where you're at' position. And the person who remains aloof, detached and emotionally cold in every situation, or the one who constantly cracks jokes and uses humour to deal with *everything* is stuck in the 'detached observer' position.

CONFIDENCE TRICK: Influencing Positions

- Influence others through checking their position and matching yours to it. You're unlikely, unless they are extremely inquisitive about you, to spend too much time in the 'where I'm at' position. Use the 'where you're at' position to get them to talk about themselves, and if they appear to be quite detached and analytical move to the 'detached observer' position with them.

- Whenever you are in a situation where you feel you're not getting through to people, check your position – how stuck you are in it and whether you should move. How would you think and feel if you were in one of the other positions? For instance, if you are overcome with shyness at a meeting, what are the other people thinking and feeling? It is likely they are bringing a range of concerns and experiences with them. It is also likely that there are some people there who feel very similar to the way you do. Putting yourself in the detached observer position, you may observe that this is *just* a meeting, where quite a lot of people lack direction as to how to behave and what to say. The event itself may then appear insignificant.

- Act out situations where you feel you're not getting through to people. Take three chairs, and make them represent each position. In the 'where you're at' position, work out how you think and feel about the problem. Then move to the 'where the other person's at' position. In this instance it might be your boss you're having problems with. What does she/he think and feel about you and this problem? Then move to the 'detached observer' position, and take up an overview of the situation. What exactly is going on and how can the deadlock be resolved?

This three-position notion is a very simple and extremely useful idea. We can use it in every situation where we communicate with others. For instance, we can check that we've not got 'stuck' in the letters we write. That is, we are expressing our own opinions, showing understanding of the other person's position, and also that we include some detached analysis. When people looked glazed as we witter on about ourselves, we can give ourselves a mental note to move from 'where we're at' to 'where they're at'. If we are talking about something controversial, and we don't know how our listeners are responding, then we can move into 'detached observer' mode and ask them what do they think, so far.

Language indicates the position you're in. If your talk is littered with 'What I think', 'What I believe', 'I know', 'I'm of the opinion', then you are clearly expressing your own concerns. When you use phrases like, 'We could', 'You possibly', 'You probably', 'I don't know if you feel the same', 'What's your opinion?' then you're moving to the other person's position. And when clear statements of commentary, analysis and evidence-seeking come in, like 'The party's getting crowded', 'Everyone's talking at once', and 'I don't feel that I'm getting through to you – is that true?' then you are wearing the detached observer's hat.

It can be useful, when you're on the phone or at meetings to doodle with a paper and pen, around the three positions. Listen out for other people shifting around between the three positions, as well as being aware of how you shift around them, yourself. Notice how a professional role can affect the position taken. In training doctors, for instance, I've noticed how the great majority of them answer almost all questions from the position of detached observer. Understandable, when you think of the type of job they do. But too much taking up of the detached observer position can mean that influence is weakened. In group discussion, personal conviction and understanding of other people's positions count for much in wielding influence.

Seeing, hearing, feeling

We process our experiences of the world through our senses, and as individuals, some senses take greater priority than others. So some of us respond visually much of the time, making sense of events through pictures in our minds. Others prefer to process auditorily, being more responsive to what they hear, and the sound of dialogue within their minds. Others prefer to respond kinaesthetically, responding to what they feel, both in terms of what they touch, and their emotions.

Of course, we don't respond exclusively through one channel. If our senses are fully functioning, we use all three. But, as individuals, we have decided preferences: 'We trust one door more than the others.' (Genie Laborde, author of *Influencing with Integrity*).

Visual processing   How do we know which channel we prefer? Well, those of us who prefer the visual will always like to make pictures in our minds. We'll tend to move and talk quickly, as thinking in terms of pictures is quicker than thinking auditorily, in terms of sounds, or kinaesthetically, in terms of feelings. When we're learning or being sold anything, we'll prefer to be shown rather than told. If we're starting off on a project, we will need to visualise what progress and the finished result will look like. Our clothes may be especially expressive of how we are feeling – dressing stylishly when we are are on *top form*, but adopting a more low-key style when preoccupied with a challenge.

Certain patterns of eye movement can indicate that a person is a visual. Visually receptive people tend to move their eyes upwards to the right and the left, and to look straight ahead, slightly defocused, when they are picturing their ideas. They also tend to breathe quite rapidly, using the upper part of the chest.

CONFIDENCE TRICK: Seeing Influence

- To influence someone who is predominantly visual, use pictures, diagrams, visualisations of how things will look in the future. You are then talking to them using a frame of reference they understand.

- Appropriate use of language, too, can help build connections and access to your ideas. For the obviously visually oriented person, phrases like 'I see your point of view' and 'let me put you in the picture' and 'what is your perspective on all this?' will make a great deal of sense.

Auditory processing Those of us who prefer to use sound to process the world, will tend to be extremely sensitive to background sound. We will enjoy talking (perhaps, too much) and excel at communicating over the 'phone. We will prefer to be told, rather than shown. We will be quick to gather large amounts of information from the spoken word, whereas our visual and kinaesthetic colleagues can be left behind. When we're working on a project, we will have a strong internal dialogue going on inside our heads, talking over progress. We may enjoy relaxing by listening to music or new age relaxation tapes.

Auditorily responsive people tend to move their eyes to the right and left on a level. Their eyes will look downwards to the left, too. They breathe lower down in the chest than visuals, and their movement and speech may be characterised by a steady, easy rhythm.

CONFIDENCE TRICK: Hearing Influence

- To influence someone who prefers to respond auditorily, we need to concentrate on how we sound and what we say. We should make our voices sound as interesting as possible.

- Again, use of language can help to build a connection: 'I hear you', 'That sounds terrific', and 'It needs some fine-tuning', are all examples of phrases that might be used by and can appeal to the auditorily sensitive person.

Kinaesthetic processing Finally, kinaesthetic types. Because feelings are important to kinaesthetics, they will be keen on sensing motives and emotions behind communication. As kinaesthetics, when genuine emotion is conveyed to us, we will respond well to it. We may be quite tactile with other people, and when we're involved in a project we will take a 'hands-on' approach. We like to touch that which we are interested in buying. With our orientation towards feeling good, we may particularly enjoy exercise and sensual delights such as massage and aromatherapy.

We may have low voices, and breathe very deeply and slowly. Our sensitivity may come through in our listening skills. We will make it easy for others to express their feelings. Our eyes will look down to the right quite often.

CONFIDENCE TRICK: Feeling Influence

- To influence and connect with someone who is predominantly kinaesthetic, we need to touch their feelings. We need to create the idea of how people would feel if our plans were implemented.

- Suitable use of language will also help you get through to the kinaesthetically oriented: 'How do you feel about this?', 'I can handle it', 'Let's hold on to that idea', and, 'Is this a touch subject?' are likely to have a good impact on them. They also respond well to metaphors: when something is described as being like something else, in order to conjure up sensation. We could say, for instance, that a project we want to start, might 'feel like embarking on an exciting journey with an unknown destination . . .'

Mirror, Mirror . . .

There are four aspects of communication which we have covered in Chapter Three, that are considered important in NCP:

- Awareness of the results we want.

- Sensitivity to how we respond to and process the world.

- How adaptable we can make our body language, movement, facial expression, eye contact and voice (covered in Chapters Six and Twelve).

- Rapport. This final quality is considered the most important by many, so I will discuss it in detail here.

What is rapport?   Well, it implies harmony, connection, empathy and trust. It is seeing parts of ourselves in other people. And, like catching a glimpse of yourself in a mirror when you're looking good, it is immensely satisfying. We build rapport through gauging the other person's preference for the visual, auditory and kinaesthetic channels and responding accordingly. We can help ourselves find out their preference by encouraging them to describe experiences: 'How did you find it there? How did you like that? What was that like?' Rapport building is essential for social and business success, and confidence.

We can also build rapport through 'mirroring' other people. What we do here, is to reflect back to the other person aspects of their body language, movement, eye contact, and use of voice. So, if we are sitting opposite someone who's leaning backwards in a very expansive position, we adjust our own position so that it is similar to theirs. When we are with someone who talks in a quick high voice, and our own way of speaking is in a slow, low voice, then we adjust our speaking voice to make it closer to theirs. We can even adjust our breathing so that it is in closer harmony with the other person's.

There are some obvious dangers in doing this. You could look and sound like you are facetiously mimicking the other person, or patronising them. This would destroy any rapport that already exists. Mirroring has to be done with skill and subtlety if it is to work. So you could choose to use 'crossover' mirroring: that is, if the person you're with keeps pushing their glasses up with their right hand, then you could mirror that gesture by touching your cheek occasionally with your left hand. With someone who uses a great deal of quick jerky movement, pacing up and down while they talk with you, then you may want to subtly tap out their changes of direction using foot tapping, finger drumming, or pencil twiddling. The aim really, is to establish underlying rhythms (which all of us have in our movement and speech) in harmony.

We can also mirror one another very effectively through use of language. For instance, let's say you want some money from your head of department to develop a new project. His objection to it is: 'I've spent money on this sort of thing before, and it's led nowhere.' You could reflect back on what he's said: 'You've spent money on this sort of thing before and it's led nowhere. But can you now see a possibility of a project like this working?' (or '. . . does it sound like it could work?' or '. . . do you get a sense that it could work?'). This is quite different from retorting with a, 'But this is quite different from what's gone before.' By mirroring what he says, you take him along with you, before gently suggesting that he looks to the future.

We can maintain rapport while challenging the views and opinions of others. One of the best ways to challenge others is to ask them questions about the specifics of what they mean and intend: 'What do you mean by "fair" specifically?', 'What does "quality" mean exactly?' and, 'When you say you intend to develop the team, how will you do that specifically?' We can soften the challenge by preceding it with phrases such as 'I'm interested in . . .', or 'Would you mind telling me', or 'It makes me wonder what . . .' The toughest questions to avoid are often those that start with 'why'.

When we maintain rapport with the other person, through sensitive behaviour, then we continue to support their identity as a person. Our challenge is to their argument, and not to who they are. We can disagree and yet continue to build a relationship.

*N*egotiating – *Getting Chunky*

This approach has some useful techniques to offer negotiators. And of course all of us perform this role at some time or another: at work, when we buy houses, and in our relationships with friends and family. It suggests that we can use language to help us discuss differences, get agreement and strengthen rather than destroy relationships.

Chunking up When we are stuck in a negotiation, we should 'chunk up'. This means that we should move from the specifics to a general category. This is likely to involve words which are open to a variety of meanings: like recognition, status, power, freedom and equality. Please see, hear and sense what I mean.

Arnold has asked his boss, Ruth, for a pay rise. They cannot agree over how much Arnold should be given. Ruth asks Arnold:

'What does this pay rise mean to you?' To which he replies, 'Well, it would show that you think I'm valuable.' And Ruth clarifies, 'So the money is about recognition of your abilities and experience?' Arnold agrees. Ruth then asks Arnold if there is any other way he could get this recognition. He suggests a change of job title. They settle on a pay rise mid-way between what the two of them wanted, along with a new job title for Arnold. They have both got some of what they wanted and they both feel their relationship is improved.

Chunking down When we want to get specifics sorted out, we need to 'chunk down' – move from the general to the more specific, so that our language is likely to become tighter and less open to many interpretations. So, for instance, if Ruth and Arnold are locked into debate over whether Arnold should be given a pay rise at all, to find out specifically what he wants, Ruth will ask Arnie, 'How would your life be different if you had a pay rise?' To which he replies, 'I'd feel more important.' (Here, we are back with our contrasting and comparing themes discussed in Chapter Two.)

Good negotiators frequently move to the 'detached observer' position, to let the other person know what is going to happen next: 'Let me make a suggestion', and 'What I'm going to ask you next may surprise you'. They often give reasons followed by proposals, which is less abrupt than the other way around: 'The project has run out of backers. So I'm proposing to ask you to increase your contribution', is softer than 'I'm proposing to ask you to increase your contribution, as the project has run out of money.' Above all, good negotiators maintain rapport and constructive relations by emphasising areas of agreement.

Anchoring

Our final technique is known as 'anchoring'. Anchors can be used to make ourselves or other people feel differently. They work in the same way that our responses are affected by a certain expression on our boss's face or a particular tone of voice from our partner. These 'anchors' change the way we felt when we walked into the room. Anchors are said to bring back strong emotional feelings connected with a previous event. They can be visual, like adopting a certain position, facial expression or eye movement. They can be auditory, like coughing, throat clearing, 'mmn', an intimate tone of voice, or a specific word. They can be kinaesthetic, such as a touch on the arm, a squeeze of the elbow, a hand on the shoulder.

CONFIDENCE TRICK: Anchoring Ourselves and Others

- For anchors to work, they must be set in place by recollecting a situation where you felt a clear emotional response, and they must be easy to recall. Take a situation where you felt really confident. Recall how you looked, sounded and felt in that situation. Really enjoy this. Now perform your anchor: it might be a look at your watch, a hum or a sigh, or a gesture that you feel, like making a circle with your thumb and forefinger. Recall your state of confidence three times and each time perform your anchor to lodge it in your mind. The next time you feel shyness coming on, use your anchor to return you to this confident state.

- We can anchor other people to certain responses. Let's say you're having a meeting in a boardroom, and the chairperson's seat remains vacant. If you sit there for the duration of the meeting, and the others present are used to responding to a higher-status figure in that chair, you will be accorded more respect and recognition than if you sat elsewhere.

Framework 2: Transactional Analysis

In the late 1960s, two books on psychology became enormous best sellers, first in the USA and then in Britain. These were *Games People Play*, by Eric Berne; and *I'm Ok – You're Ok*, by Thomas Harris. Both of these books were about transactional analysis. A transaction is an act of communication, a stimulus from one person and a response from another. So these books were about our relationships and how we communicate with one another.

The framework described in these books said that we all have parts of our personalities, or ego states, which correspond with the roles of parent, adult and child. Through our behaviour with one another we act out these personality parts. When you are coolly rational while solving a problem at work, then your *adult* is in control. When you are rolling around on the floor and giggling helplessly with your children at home, then (although you are there as their parent) the *child* part of your personality has come out to play. When you catch sight of yourself in a mirror and inwardly admonish: 'I should know better at my age', the *parent* in you is coming to the fore.

This parent/adult/child framework was originally developed by psychiatrists. Now it is used in all sorts of contexts and has won widespread

Parent and Child Roles

credibility because it has great common sense appeal. As the types of behaviour it describes are so immediately recognisable, it is especially suitable for helping people communicate more effectively. And again, I'm presenting a few ideas here. If you would like to know more, please refer to the reading list.

The parent

The parent part of a personality divides into two: *Nurturing parent and Critical parent.*

We are using our nurturing parent when we show understanding and concern for ourselves and for others. Our behaviour will be sensitive and conciliatory; we will look at the other person to see how they are reacting and we will speak fairly softly. Our body language will indicate interest and attention. We will recall – though not always consciously – how our own parents cared for and nurtured us as infants.

Critical parent, on the other, will remind us of our rogue rules, all those shoulds and musts and must nots. When we are in a critical parent state, then we can be heavily critical of ourselves and of other people. As we grew up, many of us will have heard messages that made us feel we, as individuals, are intrinsically bad, rather than that some aspects of our behaviour presented the problem. These are the messages that govern the critical parent role. Critical parent behaviour is charac-terised by upright and uptight body language, a rigid and disapproving facial expression and a tense or clipped voice. Finger wagging, as you might expect, is also common. The critic may generalise and exaggerate in order to make the other person really feel the strength of their disapproval.

The adult

Adult behaviour, again as you might expect, is characterised by rationality, logic and thought. The adult part of our personalities is the one that processes information, that stores facts and experiences, that examines possibilities. Adult behaviour will be characterised by calmness, with open but not over-expansive body language. There will not be very much facial expression, and our voices will sound reasonable and relaxed, rather than hugely enthusiastic or tense and angry.

Our 'adults' tell us how to do things. Whereas in parent state, we respond as we've been taught; and in child state, we respond as we happen to feel, in adult state we respond in accordance with what we've figured out for ourselves. It's often an aim of transactional analysis to get people to use their adult more before they act. That's not to deny the importance of emotions – our nurturing parent and child states are also valuable for psychological health, but they should not take precedence.

The child

Like the parent part of our personality, the child divides into different aspects.

- Natural child.
- Adapted child.

Our natural child is curious, spontaneous and says what we want and need. This is the part of us that uses humour, plays and has fun. It expresses our feelings and is creative. Natural child behaviour will be characterised by lots of animation in movement and facial expression, and uninhibited, enthusiastic responses.

The adapted child part of our personality has been heavily influenced by parental messages, and in this role, we can act as *compliant child* or *rebellious child.* When we're playing compliant child, we will use defensive body language, have an apologetic expression, and talk too quietly, with hesitation. We will be responding unconsciously to commands from the past such as: 'Shut up!', 'Don't ask so many questions!' and 'Do as you're told!'

In contrast, when we play rebellious child, we are responding against messages from our parents. As rebellious children, we may continue using behaviour that is destructive – for instance we may continue to abuse drugs or alcohol when our nurturing parent is telling us that we could take better care of ourselves. Rebellious child behaviour is characterised by defiant body language, pouting facial expression, and a tone of voice that reminds the listener of a naughty little child.

Why do we stay 'not OK'?

From the descriptions above, it will be clear that some states are happier than others. Life goes more smoothly when we are behaving as adults, nurturing parents, and natural children. Other people respond to us well. However, when we frequently play the roles of critical parent, compliant or rebellious child, then we can end up feeling confused, frustrated, angry and bitter. We will almost certainly have relationship problems.

Transactional analysis talks about the idea of 'strokes'. These are units of recognition – an acknowledgement from another person of our existence. We can discover early on that some behaviour is rewarded more often with 'strokes' than other behaviour. For instance, a small child may get more attention from his mother when he's naughty and rebellious, than when he entertains himself by playing in a self-sufficient way. As children, when we are told off by our parents, or see one parent criticising the other, we may realise that critical parent behaviour gets a lot of attention.

So we keep using behaviour from our critical parent and adapted child that is destructive. It is better for us to gain attention for the negative, than to go without attention at all. For without attention we psychologically – and often physically – die.

Curtailing conflict

An understanding of how we shift from one state to another (i.e. adult, parent, child), can be very useful in preventing conflict developing. Let's say two people at work, Sue and Bill, are both in critical parent mode – meaning trouble brewing:

SUE: 'Bill, did you take that report down to head office?'

BILL: 'Um, no. It's your responsibility, I believe.'

SUE: 'Hang on, no it's not. You're supposed to do it . . .'

Bill sees trouble brewing and wisely shifts into nurturing parent: 'Mnn. I can see you're concerned about this . . .' And then into adult: 'I think it would be a good idea if I took it down there now. I'll phone them to apologise for the delay. When I get back, shall we sort out who's meant to do it?'

Nurturing parent is always a useful role to adopt when people are getting angry, upset or critical. For instance, if they are playing rebellious child and sulking in the office:

SUE: 'I'm not talking about it any more . . . it's just not fair that I have to do everything.'

BILL: 'I can understand why you're peeved. Do you want to tell me exactly what you're having to do?'

Alternatively, Bill could have responded through using his natural child: 'Sue you look really tragic. I'm dying for a drink. D'you fancy one?'

SUE: (laughing) 'Oh, all right . . .'

Remember:

As nurturing parents, we attend to feelings: shame, fear, anger and grief.

As adults, we appeal to the other person's adult, and their powers of deduction and reasoning.

As natural children, we are inquisitive, humorous, playful and impulsive.

So when someone is being *negatively critical and judgemental about you* and playing **critical parent**, take up the role of **nurturing parent**, showing concern and understanding, and/or **adult**, using reason and logic.

When the other person is playing **compliant** child, and *avoiding responsibility, not contributing at all to meetings or handling complaints and aggressive people badly*, take up the role of **natural child**, being spontaneous, uninhibited and assertive (humour is useful, too), and/or **adult**, using reason and logic.

When someone is *sulking, refusing to co-operate, intent on having their own way or trying to get others to be **rebellious children***, too, take up the role of ***natural child***, being spontaneous, uninhibited and assertive, and/or ***nurturing parent***, using concern and understanding again.

CONFIDENCE TRICK: Changing Roles

These ideas from transactional analysis become most useful when we see people acting these roles in everyday life.

- Keep your eyes and ears open for people who are clearly acting out these different parts. Some people play some parts so frequently that they become locked into that role: the fifty-year-old woman who dresses in baby pinks and blues and has a breathy, baby voice; the twenty-year-old man going on sixty, who appears old before his time and sounds critical and rigid.

- Do you have a relationship that is frequently awkward? If so, work out what happened the last time you met, in terms of parent/adult/child interaction. What role did the other person play? Can you change the role you took? What would you say and do in your new role? Rehearse your behaviour and lines aloud with a clear idea of the new role you are playing.

Game Spotting

Transactional analysis also developed the idea that we play psychological games with one another. Dr Stephen Karpman suggested that some of the most common roles we take revolve around a triangle – with the roles of victim, persecutor and rescuer at separate points. We move around the triangle and play different roles as the game progresses. Let me give you an example:

George manages a team and one of its members, Stephanie, pays very little attention to what he says. She is in the role of persecutor and George is the victim. Fed up with what he sees as her insubordination, George reports Stephanie, to *his* boss, Anne. George is now persecuting his victim, Stephanie. Anne decides to rescue Stephanie by befriending her and finding out her problems. In the role of rescuer and in siding with Stephanie, Anne becomes George's persecutor. He's back as victim again. When George sees Stephanie to discuss what's happened, and Stephanie says she thinks Anne's interfered too much, then Ann is turning into the victim.

This triangle is a dangerous game to get into, as there is a strong likelihood of ending up in the victim position at some point. It's what happens to the sons, daughters, husbands and wives of alcoholics. They start off as rescuers, persecute a bit perhaps, and often finish up being victims, as much, if not more than the alcoholics themselves. In the same way, women who sacrifice themselves for their families, and spend a lot of time rescuing their husbands and children, often end up persecuting them in later life, or feeling like abandoned victims.

Other well-known games people play

These are too numerous to set down in any detail here, so I've selected some of the ones most relevant to this book.

Kick me   This is where the game-player plays the victim and invites you to persecute or rescue them. You may know someone who plays this game. She/he may be the sort of person who always has a lot of problems she/he wants to talk to you about. Or she/he may always be late for meetings, so that you can feel irritated with her or him. She/he will find all sorts of ways of putting herself/himself down, in search of negative strokes, and will be rewarded by the reaction you give. *Kick Me* will often lead into another game:

Why don't you ... yes but   When you go on courses, you will often find people who play this game with the trainer. What the game-player does is to present the trainer with as many problems as she/he can. If the trainer is not wise to the game, then she/he will try and solve the problems. But at every turning the game-player has a 'yes but'. The game-player is persecuting the trainer and getting a reward by shaming them. Like this:

GAME PLAYER: 'How can I feel more confident in speaking?'

TRAINER: 'You can look at what messages you are giving yourself.'

145

GAME PLAYER: 'Yes but, I don't think it is psychological.'

TRAINER: 'Then perhaps you could have voice lessons.'

GAME PLAYER: 'Yes but, I've done all that.'

TRAINER: 'How about joining a drama club?'

GAME PLAYER: 'Yes but, I wouldn't say anything.'

and so on . . . You can see how this game gets going very rapidly, if the unwitting victim falls into the trap of being too keen to rescue the game-player.

What's happening here, is that the game-player is trying to fool the other person into coming to rescue them. The game-player then moves from apparent victim into persecutor, so that the other person ends up being the real victim.

This final game says it all really, in its title:

NIGYSOB (Now I've got you, you son of a bitch) American-isms aside, this game involves the game-player persecuting the victim by trying to discover his or her mistakes and inconsistencies. Sometimes, people play this by firing lots of questions at the victim, until they find one that can't be answered. Then they crow victoriously to themselves 'Nigysob!' In another instance, it could be routine for you to present your boss with reports that you take a great deal of time and trouble over. Your boss will search for something to rumble you about – be it a minor spelling mistake or the layout of the page. In yet another instance, a manager may play this when she/he sees something going wrong with a project and deliberately doesn't mention it until it's too late. Or the same manager may ask someone to do something they have failed at several times before, knowing they will fail again.

This game is obviously going to appeal to people who feel insecure about their own strengths and abilities. They will lie in wait until they can rumble their victims, and in so doing get temporary relief from their own hang-ups.

CONFIDENCE TRICK: Spoilsporting

- Have you been involved in games that have undermined your confidence? Have you rescued people only to end up as victim? Can you work out what you will say and do next time you're drawn into such a game? Here are some of my own suggestions, to set you thinking. We can stop playing games in any of the following ways:

- Not giving the game-player the reward they want. So we don't rush in to get annoyed or extremely concerned with *Kick Me* players. We allow *Why don't you ... yes, but* players to solve their own problems. If we suspect we are being set up to play *NIGYSOB* then we don't bat an eyelid when we are rumbled – it really doesn't matter to us.

- We confront the game-player. This works especially with *NIGYSOB*. Asking very casually, and perhaps with some humour, whether the game-player's intention is to rumble you. Or, in adult mode, we can talk in a very detached way about what is going on.

- We hold back from rushing in to give advice. Perhaps the game-player can get advice from other sources, or find their own solutions.

- People are less likely to bother to play *Why don't you ... yes but* and *NIGYSOB* if you avoid the God role and admit that you are not a complete authority on everything. If we have a sense of humour about ourselves and our role, and don't take ourselves too seriously, then others are less likely to want to rumble us. That's not to say it won't ever happen.

- In business and in our personal lives, it can be very useful to establish contracts between ourselves. We all do this informally and unconsciously. When relationships are a problem, it can be very helpful to ask yourself 'Do this person and myself have a clear and mutually compatible understanding of what we both want to get out of the relationship?'

- Sometimes, too, we need to sit down and negotiate with the other person exactly what these rules are. We need to tell them how we feel, what the effects of their game-playing are, and what we want to be done differently. Ask them what they want and then negotiation can begin.

10 *Dealing with Stress*

**CONFIDENCE KEY: Causes of stress,
reducing stress, curbing 'drivers'**

IN THIS chapter we look at causes of stress, how we know when we're under stress, what we can do about it, and how we can deal with our 'drivers' – the tendencies we have to behave in certain ways under pressure.

Causes of Stress

A lack of confidence – that feeling that things are out of control and we can't cope – is a major cause of stress. And all of us can fall prey to it, be we housewives, shop assistants, computer analysts or company directors. A growing awareness that this is so, has meant that stress has become much more widely talked about. Yet it is still a dirty word in many a British stiff-upper-lipped organisation: perhaps in part due to the fact that, from the employers' point of view, stress causes damage through absenteeism and poor performance on the job. Macho working values and a recession-based fear of unemployment have meant that many of us are now used to experiencing stress at work, and not feeling able to do anything about it. But if we persist in ignoring stress we may become seriously ill, in which case our personal and professional lives may suffer.

Imbalance is usually a feature of stress. We may have too much to do, and too little time; too much freedom, and too little direction; too much responsibility, and too little power. And change can often create a strong sense of imbalance: what we were in control of goes out of control, and our security may seem threatened. The more we know about ourselves, the quicker we are able to define fresh frameworks that make us feel secure again.

How we respond as individuals to life's challenges varies widely. What some will regard as horribly stressful, others will find exhilarating. So perception affects our response, and much of what's been covered in previous chapters of this book is relevant here. Recalling Chapter Two, constantly using rogue rules such as: 'I must always do better than everyone else', can cause stress. Realistically, you *can't* always do better. In Chapter Three, we studied constructs – using pairs of contrasting ideas as 'rulers' or 'measures' to interpret events – and saw that over-using certain measures creates problems. Always reading situations with a strong: 'How am I superior? . . . How are others treating me as inferior?' measure will eventually become extremely stressful. A measure of: 'How do I connect? . . . What are the differences between us?' will be more useful.

Also in Chapter Three I described how role over- and under-load can cause frustration (and stress). Having too many parts to play or insufficient challenge within a specific role. As for types (and type-casting), well, common sense will tell us that intuitive, feeling, perceiving extroverts will suffer stress in jobs where they need to judge, to analyse, to persevere with detailed tasks, while spending much of their time working alone! Knowing our personality preferences can help us be square pegs in square holes, and thus avoid such a recipe for stress unlimited.

Moving on to this middle section of *Total Confidence*, we have seen how a lack of assertive communication skills can cause stress. If we can't say what we want and need, then we'll inevitably become frustrated. Ideas from NLP (Chapter Nine) can help us to reduce stress by showing us how to increase rapport with others, and how to use 'anchors', instant reminders of relaxed states. In the same chapter, the parent/adult/child model from transactional analysis teaches us that it is not helpful to get stuck in one type of behaviour. When we overdose on being the rational, decision-taking adult, for instance, we can do so at the expense of caring for ourselves as nurturing parent, or having fun and being creative as natural child.

What Stress Is

I don't know about you, but whenever I read a list of stress symptoms,

I feel that I'm experiencing most of them. Where do these symptoms come from? What is stress?

Well, our genes have programmed our stress response. To ensure continued survival when faced with danger we react with what is known as 'the fight or flight' response. Blood pumps faster around the body, food is quickly turned into energy, our muscles prepare for action and we become highly sensitive and aware of stimuli. This was a fine state to be in when we had to fight a mammoth or flee from a dinosaur. But unfortunately our bodies have not adjusted this stress response in keeping with the very different pressures of modern life. And whereas in the Stone Age we speedily discharged the pent-up energy created by this response, in today's world we do not. Instead, we store stress in our bodies and minds as distress; and it builds up as more problems accrue.

When we *do* discharge stress effectively though – by appropriately expressing our tension and frustration – it can be a useful reaction. The stress response can help us to perform more effectively, provided it is not allowed to build up in our system. We need to dispense with the stuff, rather than storing it in our minds and bodies. When we know how to handle our stress, we can seek out and cope with challenge, with confidence.

A stimulating amount of challenge – which is often another word for 'problem' or 'stress' – can make us: work more efficiently; get new ideas and take more risks; have more energy and look better; feel fine on less sleep – and enjoy sex more; feel important; feel fit and assertive; have more confidence and more enthusiasm. In short, having lots of stimulation and coping with it, we thrive on our busyness.

But when stress becomes too much, we can make wrong decisions and become snappy and irritable; experience dramatic mood swings; have trouble sleeping, or sleep more than usual; avoid seeing friends and doing things. We smoke more, drink more alcohol and coffee; eat to excess – or not enough and have a whole range of physical symptoms such as head-, back- and neck-ache; lapses of memory and loss of concentration; stomach upsets and panic attacks.

Signs in our behaviour that we may be under stress include: lots of blinking, fidgeting, talking incessantly, frowning unconsciously, repeated swallowing or licking of the lips, making obsessive notes – in our heads or on paper. We may also display all sorts of phobias, or addictions.

CONFIDENCE TRICK: Stress Measures

Often, when we are under stress, we become very blinkered about our situation and fail to consider all the available options. The rather calculating process described in this Confidence Trick can help us avoid this tendency and be more tactical in our approach.

- Take three events, and or people, that you find stressful. Jot them down on a piece of paper, each one heading up a column.

- Think about each one of these stressors. What are these events and relationships giving you too much or too many of? Jot down your answers in each column. Then ask yourself what are these stressors giving you too little or too few of?

- Having analysed the imbalance, you now need to choose an approach to deal with each one of these. Basically, there are three different approaches you can take:

1. You can change the way you interpret and react to the situation. Your use of rogue rules and/or constructs may need some attention.

2. You can change the event and/or the way other people are interpreting and reacting. This is often more challenging than changing your own responses, but it can be done. You will find it useful to review how you are using communication skills and techniques of assertiveness.

3. You can walk away from the situation, and/or relationship. Sometimes a situation or relationship may be so bad, that there is no other route available than the one marked 'exit'. Then, at least, you will 'live to fight another day'. This is particularly relevant advice for those of us who obsessively stick with things – the persistent, tenacious and single-minded.

Self-motivated Stress

So far in this chapter we have dealt with stress largely in terms of external factors – but what about the stress we create for ourselves? Most of us, if we give it a moment's thought, will agree that we do drive ourselves. Why do we do it? How can we stop?

Abandoning the driving seat

We put ourselves under stress when we drive ourselves to achieve, to care for our families completely, to have utterly fulfilling relationships or to live a fantasy lifestyle as defined by the media – particularly via advertising. Transactional analysis has described how these drives cause us to have certain behavioural tendencies. And these tendencies or 'drivers' may have developed out of messages we received from others in the past: be good, be kind, be giving – be perfect.

On training courses people readily identify one or two drivers that they know and respond to. These 'drivers' are not all bad; indeed, each one has strengths. Recognising them, though, can help us when they are causing us to career out of control. Here are some of the main drivers and ways in which we can keep them in check.

Hurry up

You'll often hear people with a 'hurry up' tendency saying things like 'We said we'd get there early', 'Be with you in a second', 'Let's get a move on . . .' Hurry Ups get things done quickly, like tight deadlines and pressure, and enjoy feeling that they are efficiently dealing with several things at once.

If you've a strong Hurry Up tendency, you may appear impatient, you may move, talk and eat quickly and prefer to do these activities all together at the same time. You may be fidgety and finish other people's sentences for them – helpful from your point of view, but irritating, even patronising for the speaker. Hurry Ups never seem to have enough time to cram in all they need to do. At the end of an appointment, they often need to rush off to the next engagement in an over-crowded schedule.

If you are a Hurry Up you can create difficulties for other people who work and live with you, too. Though you may have every confidence in your ability to produce what's required, however little notice you're given, your colleagues may find your philosophy of time stressful, especially when they prefer to work at a steady, slower pace. For people who prefer to avoid too much drama, and who like to plan thoroughly and in detail, life with you can be a nightmare. They'll feel nervous and edgy.

As a human Concorde who gets addicted to this tendency, you can end up feeling permanently frazzled and as though nothing is under your control. Hurry Ups can help themselves work to a different rhythm through using long term planning, dividing the long term plan into smaller sections, so they can regularly review progress and adjust direction, if necessary. Hurry Ups need to ensure they allocate time to quiet, reflective activities such as thinking, meditating and reading. A leisure time activity which involves sorting out and dealing with small detail, will offer a different perspective.

In communication, you need to slow down and listen, letting others talk at their own pace, and finish for themselves what they want to say . . . Relax. You may hear things to your advantage.

Try hard

Try Hards will often be heard to use phrases like 'I'll do it', 'What a great idea', 'I'll volunteer', 'I'll help with that'. They are enormously enthusiastic, which makes them popular with others, and they always have plenty of invitations to get involved in work and social projects. People with this tendency love to be confronted with a problem, because they're usually good at problem solving – they consider all the possible consequences of a solution. Try Hards spread themselves wide with a thoroughly holistic approach.

You can spot Try Hards by the way they listen with animated interest, and that puppy dog look on their faces. Try Hards often regard it as important to throw themselves into life, so you will find them laughing loudly and being very expressive. They think it's crucial to do the right thing, which can lead them to being impulsive. Like my friend, who on approaching thirty decided she had to get married. Within three months of meeting 'Mr Will-do', rather than 'Mr Right', she married him. And yes, you've guessed it: six months later they were in the divorce courts.

As a Try Hard, you may have more of a sense of being a passenger in your own life, albeit a very responsive one, than a driver. You need to shift perspective to see yourself as having greater control and resources, and long-term staying power. Focus is what Try Hards lack. Once you've got something off the ground, you may find yourself getting distracted and failing to see the project through to conclusion. Because you are easily sidetracked, you get lost in irrelevant detail. In conversation, you will go off at tangents, have a distracted air, and even appear to evade questions. The danger is that while admiring your generosity of spirit, people might not take you seriously because of your apparent lack of clear intention and depth.

Life can be frustrating if your Try Hard tendency is taking over. You need to think about planning things, so that you have a very clear through line. Make sure that you know when you will be finishing something, as well as when you will be starting your next project. Limit yourself in what you volunteer for, so that you do have some time for yourself. And when you are working on something and getting involved in detail, or going off at tangents, keep asking yourself: 'Is this really necessary?' Bear in mind that your tendency is going to encourage people to ask you to get involved in lots of things and you need to learn to say 'No'. Resolve to set aside time for a leisure activity – and let someone else volunteer for a change.

Too much of a Try Hard tendency can also mean that whenever you do something you've not done before, then you worry about 'getting it right', and become fixated on results rather than process. Consider *how* you are doing things, and freeing tension. Be kind to yourself: you are good enough and don't have to try harder and harder. Ration your energy.

Be perfect

The scourge of we sloppier types, Be Perfects are recognisable by such comments as, 'That's not quite right', 'Have I dotted the "i"'s and crossed the "t"'s?', 'This isn't exactly how I saw it'. Be Perfects must get every tiny detail absolutely right, first time. They set very high standards for themselves, and often for others, too. The striving for perfection means that Be Perfect always has projects beautifully organised, and that they have an excellent reputation for accuracy and reliability.

Be Perfects may appear over-controlled when they communicate, because their inner critic is constantly commenting to them on errors of clarity. The facial expression might be a disapproving one. They may be rather precise in their speech, because they are keen to convey exactly what they mean. They may appear to be fixated with facts as these are more reliable and measurable than feelings. As a Be Perfect, you may be aware that you behave with precision, and that your body language and appearance is neat and pristine. As you love defining boundaries, you can appear almost too self-contained and self-sufficient.

However, this preoccupation with boundaries can make Be Perfects inflexible and intolerant. You may be too ready to set unrealistic standards and give negative criticism – to yourself and to others. Be Perfects can find delegation difficult and they may work themselves into the ground, believing that no one else has the requisite high standards to perform as effectively. If you are a Be Perfect, sometimes, you will get behind with projects, because of detail-fixation. Too concerned with the small print, the overall purpose will get lost.

Be Perfects can help control their tendency to set impossibly high standards, through being deliberately more indulgent and realistic with themselves and others. Get things into perspective: ask rationally what the consequences of making mistakes are – so what if a letter contains a spelling mistake sometimes? Keep asking yourself, 'What is the whole picture here?' Be Perfects need to review their criteria and priorities. While high standards may be desirable at work, do they *have* to apply to washing the car, filling the supermarket trolley and making a sandwich? Creative activities, which inevitably involve unpredictable and 'messy' periods can be good antidotes and help Be Perfects to realise that out of chaos and error can come creative solutions. Though Be Perfects themselves throw up their hands in horror at this suggestion, doing something deliberately less than perfectly can be good therapy.

Be pleasing

'Is that all right?', 'What do you think?', 'I've sort of done it like that, okay?': these are typical Be Pleasing phrases. Be Pleasing people think of others first. They intuitively know what other people want and need, and are understanding and empathetic towards them. They appear genuinely interested in others, and collaboration suits them. Be Pleasing people are sensitive, kind and considerate.

But all this pleasing can be at Be Pleasing's own expense. Avoiding conflict, speaking in a tentative, compliant manner can mean that Be Pleasing gets trodden on by others. Deep down inside, she/he may really resent the way the needs of others always take precedence. Be Pleasing allows others to interrupt, to dominate, and will shy away from expressing their own opinions and concerns. Worrying too much about what others think, Be Pleasing types can lose sense of who they are, where they are going and what they want. Attractiveness and popularity will matter too much.

Be Pleasing people often make the mistake of thinking that others want and need the same things as they do. They assume that other people will be hyper-sensitive to rejection, as they are themselves, and so they will fudge telling a subordinate they are no longer wanted on a project, to avoid hurting them. What Be Pleasing is overlooking, is that the subordinate may be jolly glad to get out of the exercise.

Often, too, Be Pleasing people will expect rewards for their altruism. In being a 'good' girl or boy, they will expect people to treat them in the same way. And life isn't always like that – by any means. They then end up feeling like doormats when their martyrdom is not reciprocated. So if you're a 'Be Pleasing', what can you do about it?

Basic assertiveness techniques are useful, as described in Chapter Eight. Work on your body language, appearance and voice signals so that you make a powerful impression. There is further advice on these aspects in later chapters. Learn to ask people directly what they want; and to express what you want. As Be Pleasing people often have a self-image that is more about reaction to others, than being self-determining, allocate thinking, research and planning time to *your* visions and goals. Take a provocative line sometimes in conversation, just for the hell of it. And remember that when we disagree with one another, we are attacking one another's behaviour, not who we are. People who openly express their opinions and are direct, are often respected and liked for being their 'own' women and men.

Be strong

If we're managers, many of us value and cultivate a Be Strong tendency, especially at work. We'll say things like: 'No problem', 'I'll take responsibility for that', and 'Leave it to me'. Here we have the British stiff upper lip. Be Strongs stay cool, calm and logical in a crisis. They never panic and have a reputation for steadiness and consistency. Showing a strong sense of fair-play and firmness will earn them the respect of others.

Be Strongs often exude power in the way they communicate. But because they never like to admit weakness – in themselves or others –

weaker mortals may feel uncomfortable revealing anxiety or concern in the face of all this stoicism. Be Strongs may be good at negotiating – reasonable, firm and consistent. As conversationalists though, their self-control can make them dull and uninvolving. They may talk about everything in a detached and impersonal way.

As a Be Strong, you may feel that you carry the buck for everything. You are over-estimating your own significance. You didn't create the universe and you are not responsible for everything that happens in it. Other people can solve problems, too. All of us have emotional needs as well as intellectual ones. You can end up being remarkably tough on yourself in denying this. Be Strongs can often finally succumb to stress in a most spectacular way; and they'll be the last people everyone else would expect this to happen to. Human rocks they may be, but years of taking on responsibility and denying their emotions will take their toll.

If being too strong is causing *you* strain, dare to show a little human 'weakness' and develop the habit of asking other people for help. Also, find some activity that allows you to vent your emotions – be it by playing squash or the singing of arias. Find activities where you can let the child in you come out, where you are not expected to be the responsible, competent, controlled adult. Keep time for fun and frivolity to recharge your batteries and remind yourself how similar you are to others, rather than how responsible you are for them.

*D*riving Safely

So that's it – five driving tendencies that most people recognise. Which ones are you driven by? On courses and at conferences, we have great fun working out what 'drivers' various celebrities use. Princess Diana has been described as a 'Be Perfect' and a 'Be Pleasing'; the hapless Fergie as a 'Be Pleasing' and a 'Try Hard'; and Margaret Thatcher as a 'Be Strong' and 'Be Perfect' – a tough combination.

We can use our understanding of these drivers to keep our own lives on course, and to contain stress. They can also help us appreciate what drives other people, and causes them stress.

To end this chapter on a relaxing note, here are some more self-help ways to reduce self-induced stress.

CONFIDENCE TRICK: Live a Little

Some of these ideas are deliberately lighthearted, because under stress we often take ourselves too seriously:

- List your self-driving habits. Can you lose or change any of them?

- Learn to delegate. *No-one* is indispensable.

- Give yourself a day which is just for you, where either you plan nothing at all or you plan sybaritic activities such as having a massage or watching a movie.

- Do some one-off (relatively harmless) things which you have never done before and where you feel you are surrendering control: have a giant cream meringue, sing in the street, do a parachute jump, introduce yourself to other people on public transport. Do something that makes you feel joyous about life.

- Express yourself creatively by taking up painting, writing or a craft like pottery. We are all innately creative and many of us do not express this drive.

- Express yourself physically, by taking up regular exercise, even if it's just letting your hair down to ZZ Top in the living room.

- Make space and definite arrangements for leisure time in your diary.

- Avoid too much caffeine, alcohol, nicotine and other stimulants.

- Treat food as a delight to be savoured, that makes your body feel good.

- Organise your time so that you act to fulfil your visions, as well as your goals. (Your visions are about imaginary abstract ideas of how you could live, while your goals will be tangible targets.)

- Read a guide to relaxation techniques (see book list) and

try meditation, shiatzu, aromatherapy, autogenic training, etc.

- Enjoy exercising your boundaries, where you say no to work or to relatives and friends imposing.

- Be clear about what money represents to you. Do the material goods you acquire represent your professional success, good taste or enjoyment of leisure time? Is money for you about survival, security, freedom of choice, a type of lifestyle, achievement, or power? It is easier to handle money when you know what you want from it. Alternative choices often present themselves about what we have to do to get it.

- Join an evening class in something completely disconnected with your job, e.g. Lebanese cooking, topiary or photography.

When you feel that either your stress symptoms are lasting a long time, or that you are depressed consult your doctor. You may be referred for counselling or psychotherapy. Or consult one of the organisations listed in the information section at the back of this book.

Loneliness is epidemic in our current society; increasing numbers of people live alone and community spirit is in decline. We can help ourselves to deal with loneliness by involving ourselves in activities which are satisfying in themselves: like reading, studying or painting; by getting involved in voluntary work; by seeking out people in a similar position to our own. More than this, we need to appreciate that the 'happy families' myth propagated by the colour supplements, magazines and advertisers, often bears little relation to real life.

Part Three

Projecting Confidence

11 *Non-Verbal Confidence*

SAM is to represent his government department at a reception, where he is expected to mingle with his peers from other departments and to exchange information about current progress. The prospect fills him with gloom. He is shy and doesn't like socialising with strangers. Along he goes, and has barely entered the function room when his face freezes; then, horrors, he feels one of his facial muscles starting to twitch uncontrollably . . .

Nadine goes to a job interview. She feels quite nervous and when she takes her seat in front of the interview panel, she sits with her legs crossed, her arms wrapped around the front of her body, and her head tilted downwards so that she looks dolefully out at the panel from under her long fringe. Within three or four minutes they have decided not to give her the job.

Sally is a sales executive. When she's unsure of herself and suspects other people are thinking critically of her, she avoids looking at them. Her company uses 'in the field' training, which means that a sales manager accompanies Sally on her early calls, and afterwards asks the customers what impression they have formed of her. Almost every customer says that Sally looks shifty and that they wouldn't trust her. She has literally not looked them in the eye.

Non-Verbal Signals

These are tremendously significant in conveying confidence. One estimate, for instance, says 65 per cent of the signals we send one another in conversation are visual rather than audible. Another estimate says that when we make a first impression, only 7 per cent of it is conveyed through the words we use. And because we can change our body shapes and our attitudes, if sufficiently motivated to do so, we can change any negative, non-verbal signals so that we always convey confidence. A comforting thought for those of use who, for whatever reason, have to walk into a room full of intimidating strangers.

In this chapter, then, we will look at how we can use these signals so that in situations which many of us find daunting – meeting strangers, attending interviews or meetings, and speaking in public – we exude confidence. But remember, always, that the identity of the person on the receiving end matters too. For instance, very direct eye contact can be useful with an office colleague who is trying to intimidate you. It may not work so well when your boss is asking for your ideas on how you can repair some serious mistakes that you've made. Here, too much eye-to-eye contact could suggest a defiant attitude rather than an attempt to make amends.

Move That Body

As body language is all about how we move our bodies, in this section I'm going to look at positioning and movement. I also urge you to view yourself as researchers and carry out experiments, because body language is an ideal subject in which to play this role. Try out different postures yourself, as a change from habitual ones, and observe how others respond. Notice how people position themselves and move on public transport, in the street, in pubs, restaurants and shops. The patterns of body language are a richly enjoyable subject for study, and one we should have fun with.

Here are some of the poses to look out for – and what they convey:

Expanding and contracting

Our use of body language often reflects our primitive origins. For instance, we use body language to stake out territory for ourselves and to keep others at bay. And those roles that society encourages us to play will also exert an influence. Women readers who have vainly tried to sit comfortably on the tube with their arms resting on the appropriate seat arms, while wedged between two burly men, will appreciate this point. Unconsciously, many of us expect the sexes to use body language differently.

The more space we take up, by spreading our bodies and indeed our possessions, the more we indicate to others that we are to be seen as significant. The less space we occupy, by sitting with our legs tucked in neatly, our arms folded across our bodies, our shoulders rounded and heads lowered, the more we indicate to others that we are to be seen as insignificant.

So, we need to be aware that to suggest confidence, we use body language that says 'we're happy to be seen to be significant'. This doesn't mean adopting what I call 'the Big Chief Sitting Bull' or 'Super Slob' posture: sprawling back in a chair, legs spread wide, hands folded behind your head and an arrogant expression on our face that sends out signals that you don't give a jot what others think about you.

It means that you stand tall, as though your body is suspended from the top and back of the head, by an invisible string descending from the sky. Your neck and shoulders are relaxed (check whether this is so by nodding your head gently and sensing that your shoulders drop downwards and backwards, rather than being lifted and rounded with tension). Your neck is long and head held proud, rather than looking as though expecting to have to duck blows at any minute. As you walk your arms swing loosely at your sides. When you stand your arms don't immediately go to wrap around your body in a reassuring self-cuddle; you may have one hand in a pocket, or your hands may be loosely held together in front or behind your body. If you are good at physical relaxation, you may feel and look comfortable with your arms hanging loosely at your sides. In drama schools, actors learn this is the closest position to conveying a neutral attitude that they can aim to achieve.

Using the body language of relaxed expansiveness, we avoid making ourselves look too contained, too neat and tidy. Too much symmetry can suggest we are ill-at-ease, and consequently working very hard to appear on our best behaviour. Meeting strangers at parties, it is much more natural to put more weight on one leg than the other, and perhaps lean casually against a wall. In meetings, we can let one arm relax loosely on the table, while the other rests in our lap. At presentations, we can stand on quite a broad base, with our feet firmly placed on the floor, while we slightly lean our weight in one direction. In interviews, we can sit well back in the chair, with the back giving support to our spine, our legs loosely crossed and our hands resting in our laps with fingers loosely linked (good for containing shaky hands).

There is only one proviso to this advice: in situations where it is important that you show respect for the other person, neat contained body language may serve you best. Especially if you're a six-foot-three, sixteen-stone giant and the person you are attempting to ingratiate yourself with is a five-foot-two, eight-and-a-half stone stripling.

Engaging and distancing

Confident people do not feel threatened by others, so they have no need to create any form of artificial distance between themselves and others in terms of dress, posture or manner. In my company, one of our roles is to train news readers and TV presenters. A few years ago, we were asked to act as consultants on the much-publicised launch of a new channel. Though the declared aim was to create a very relaxed atmosphere, the presenters wore business dress, and were instructed to sit back and upright on the predictable peach-coloured sofa. Our advice on how they could make best use of their body language to create a friendly, relaxed atmosphere was over-ridden by technical considerations of how the set looked best and how the presenters' outfits could continue to look pristine. We were all disappointed at the restrictions imposed.

The launch was not a success. There was a rapid change of personnel and new presenters were brought in – people known for friendliness and approachability – who always leant slightly towards the camera and the interviewees. I'm sure you'll appreciate that we were pleased to have our original advice taken up in this way.

In situations like parties, interviews and presentations, where your aim is to engage with people and get more involved with them, your body language can indicate this. Lean towards them rather than away, steeple your hands together and rest them on the table, move away from a lectern so that you stand closer to your audience and are better able to connect with them.

However, in one-to-one – or small group – situations, always bear in mind that individuals have need of varying amounts of 'personal space'. That is, while some like close contact, others need to keep slightly more distance between themselves and others. Most of us are sensitive enough *not* to stand or sit too close to others, and this is especially relevant if you are physically much larger than they are, or have obvious higher status in terms of job title. If you do, you will appear intimidating.

Distancing too, has a useful function in terms of confident behaviour. When someone is standing or sitting too close to you – and not respecting your physical or psychological boundaries – then deliberately and definitely move back a step. At the same time, comment on what's going on: 'I find this position uncomfortable/overpowering/claustrophobic, so I'll just move back a little.' Be aware, too, that people often use moving back as a gesture meaning: 'This interaction is over.'

Fighting and fleeing

In Chapter Ten, I described how, under stress, we adopt what is known as the fight or flight response. This manifests itself in how we position ourselves and how we move, and while displaying some evidence of the response is only human, too much will detract from presenting a confident exterior. We see fight behaviour when a spokesperson at a meeting keeps thrusting his or head forward when speaking, banging on the table, or rising to his or her feet in protest and waving an order paper whenever they hear anything that doesn't please them.

More commonly, when confidence is low, we see flight behaviour. Quick jerky head movements, with the head dropping or flicking to the side, rather like a demented bird, lots of dancing around on the spot and fidgeting hands, are all evidence of the nervous presenter. This person clearly wants to get out of the spotlight as quickly as possible.

What can we do about these tendencies, if we have them? Well we need to become aware of the signals sent by various movements, and practise positive ones until they become automatic – cancelling out any need for former, negative ones.

What a Mover: Underlying Rhythms

We all have underlying rhythms, which influence how we move and how we speak. Fast agitated movers always talk in the same frenetic way, for instance; they never speak in languid, smooth rhythms. And when we use a lot of quick jerky movements we suggest that we have very little control over time. We seem to be performing our actions at the behest of others who we are in awe of, as we nervously rush about our tasks.

To behave in a confident way, we need to extend our range of rhythms and reactions. We can move smoothly and fluently as we glide into the party. We don't have to square up to the interviewer or audience member who asks an awkward question, or twitch like an agitated mouse at the beginning of our presentations. We can learn to vary our dances and our reactions, according to the situation and the others present.

Newsreaders, politicians and diplomats learn to behave in a way that depicts confidence, composure and authority. What can we learn from them? Well, they avoid quick jerky movements and any unnecessary gesticulating with the head or arms. They avoid tilting the head downwards and looking submissive, pulling it back and looking arrogant, tilting it sideways and looking cute, or moving it around a lot and looking flirtatious. When newsreaders are reading from autocue, they *have* to move their heads slightly so that they don't look as though they are watching a game of tennis with their eyes. But the head movement will be fluid and gentle, their whole demeanour characterised by a confident relaxed stillness.

What about the rest of the body? Well this depends on the situation. Reading the news requires the presenters to do very little with their hands, which are rarely seen. Politicians often choose to 'steeple', that it, link their hands together when they are on television. This has the advantage of hiding shaking hands, and preventing the politician performing nervous little mannerisms such as stroking their chin or smoothing their hair. To convey confidence and conviction, keep your hands well away from your face.

If you use your hands when you talk naturally, to give emphasis to certain points and to show that your whole being is involved in what you are saying, then do so when you are under scrutiny in interviews, meetings and presentations. You may find that if you try to keep your hands restrained, then your whole impression will be of someone on their best behaviour. Occasionally, however, we use our hands as compensation for language and they articulate the frustration we feel, with impatient, aggressive gestures. This is very off-putting for the person or people being addressed, and puts you in a very bad light.

CONFIDENCE TRICK: Moving Being

- In your mind's eye see, hear and feel yourself portraying confidence by your every word and gesture. In front of a mirror, look at yourself while keeping this image in mind. Do you look and feel comfortable and confident? Do the same exercise sitting down, and again look at yourself in the mirror.

- Adopt different movement images in your mind's eye. Think of yourself floating, stomping, gliding or tripping along. Then actively try out different ways of moving, especially moving with lightness and fluidity. Experiment with different actions and intentions: encouraging, welcoming, involving and reassuring. See how you can convey these through your body language.

- Improve your use of body language by taking up a gentle physical discipline such as yoga, Tai chi or body conditioning. The Alexander technique is especially useful. To use body language really effectively we need to be aware of, and in touch with, our bodies.

- If you use your hands a lot or fiddle with them, practise talking while sitting on them. This can improve your articulacy, through focusing all your energy and concentration on your speech organs.

- Going somewhere daunting? Then warm up physically beforehand, with a swim, walk, run, or by shaking out all your limbs.

Unmasking Confidence

Though it implies deception, almost all adults disguise their thoughts and feelings behind their facial expressions. Unfortunately, when our confidence drops, and we get anxious and nervous, the muscles in our faces can tighten, so our faces freeze. As the tension surges behind the mask we can feel ourselves losing control over the muscles and it becomes impossible to smile naturally. Most people's wedding photographs remind them of this. Sometimes the muscles can start to twitch uncontrollably, which is very disquieting, though only likely to be noticed by the most perceptive of observers.

Our use of facial expression can be affected by the demands of our jobs. If we have to do a lot of negotiating, as a finance manager or solicitor; or we need to detach ourselves emotionally from our jobs, as a doctor or police officer, then inscrutability will serve us very well. However, an unchanging facial expression can be very intimidating for others, especially if they are people who seek responsiveness from others. That's the majority of us, I suspect. So there are disadvantages as well as pay-offs in keeping the facial muscles set in a rigid mask. We need always to be very conscious of what expression is appropriate, and when.

Confidence is not about concealment. Even though the British generally admire stoicism and the stiff upper lip, when our faces are set in one expression, we will not succeed in sending signals to others that we are open, receptive and responsive. We will appear to be closed off and defensive. Others will not trust us readily or give us credibility.

Smile please

How do we let our masks drop? Well, the first consideration is a very practical one. We need to be sure that our teeth warrant display and inspection, and if they are not, a visit to a dentist for advice on improving them is likely to prove well worth while. The American enthusiasm for orthodontics and cosmetic dentistry perhaps partly explains why they are generally much better at smiling than we are. Then we need to learn to relax the muscles in the face, through massage, chewing gently, puckering the lips forward and pulling them backwards. Think of releasing your jaw and letting the muscles completely relax.

Perhaps the best trick is to imagine that we lip-read one another, and that the more our muscles move when we speak, the more clearly we will be understood and the better we will sound. Become aware, too, of just how softly you can speak, and yet how clear you sound, if you move your facial muscles very precisely. Practising speaking like this will make you look and sound involved and confident. But keep the pace up, so you don't begin to sound patronising. It's again a technique used by newsreaders and politicians.

The aim is to achieve a relaxed and open facial expression, rather than a clamped tense smile, or indeed, a too ready smile, either of which looks unnatural.

Jean has recently returned to work after bringing up a family. She feels that she is not being taken seriously and that though she speaks with a quite authority, a lot of her colleagues regard her as compliant and weak. When she saw herself talking on video, she quickly observed that she smiled much too much, and sometimes when it was inappropriate. Though her smile was warm and friendly, it was so frequent that it made her appear to be trying very hard to please everyone (which, of course, she was). She practised controlling and rationing her smiles until they were more appropriate to the impression she wished to convey at any particular time.

Though a dazzling smile can be a great asset, one piece of American research showed that women and men are judged differently in this area of non-verbal behaviour, too. Two groups of women and men who smiled with similar frequency, were judged by observers. The female smilers were judged to be warm and friendly, but too keen on seeking approval. The men were judged to be warm and friendly – full stop. Please don't interpret this to mean that as a woman who smiles a lot, you should become hatchet-faced. It simply illustrates the double standards that still prevail for women and men, and is worth paying attention to in the context that if you are a woman, excessive smiling may detract from your credibility.

CONFIDENCE TRICK: Preparing to Smile

- At meetings, interviews and presentations, people will be more receptive to you and assume that you are more confident and pleased to be in the situation, if you can produce a warm smile at the outset. Warm up your facial muscles beforehand, and practise smiling on a daily basis. As you walk into the room let your muscles relax into a smile, and breathe out gently through your mouth and through the smile. It's often easier to smile naturally, when we have something else to think about, as well.

- Take good care of your teeth, and if they are not in top-notch condition, seek professional advice on how to improve them. Consider any money spent in this way to be a good investment, and then display the results smilingly.

• Try this exercise from the Alexander technique, to relax your face completely. It's called the 'whispered ah'. Relax and drop your tongue to the bottom of your mouth. Tell your eyes to light up so they smile, and your cheek muscles rise. Let your jaw drop open wide and relaxed, and let the breath on a big 'ah', thinking of sighing with relief or joy.

Eye contact

As we communicate very directly with one another via our eyes, knowing how to use eye contact to convey confidence is essential. Often, when we feel nervous and self-conscious, we tend to avoid looking very much at other people. We are so sensitive to the possibility of a negative response, that we can't risk seeing them eyeing us critically. This can have several different effects: it can make us look shy and ill-at-ease, or shifty and untrustworthy, or even arrogant, in that we appear not to be much concerned about the response of others.

How should we make eye contact then? When we look at people, we should hold their gaze sufficiently long enough to acknowledge them as individuals, and to note their expression. This takes roughly about four seconds. Any quicker than that and we may appear to be glancing in cursory fashion, and we won't have sufficient time to get valuable feedback about the other person's reaction. On the other hand, if we look at people for too long, then it can appear intimidating and aggressive. As in most things, balance is important.

Who we make eye contact with, also depends on the situation. It makes good sense if we have to walk into a room full of strangers at an interview, presentation or social event, to find someone who looks friendly and to make eye contact with them for starters. Their approving response will boost our confidence. It's worth bearing in mind though, that the more we sweep the room in terms of eye contact, and the more people we look at, the greater our apparent confidence. Looking as though we are keen to communicate with the whole room, will make us appear very self-assured.

As a more advanced skill, once you're comfortable about making plenty of eye contact, you can use it tactically:

Penny is addressing a meeting. Two people are nodding encouragingly and smiling with approval. Another person looks bored, and a fourth – in this instance, the highest status person in the group – looks faintly hostile. If Penny allows her survival instinct and need to be liked to take over, then she will avoid looking at the bored and faintly hostile members of the group. She will stick with the smilers, because they are signalling that they like her. Tactically, however, this is unwise. The smilers are already indicating their approval. What Penny needs to do, is to win round the less well-disposed members of the group.

As we saw in Chapter One, we usually behave in a certain way because there are pay-offs for doing so. Pay-offs for people who sit in meetings looking bored and faintly hostile, are that they discourage or even intimidate the person doing the speaking. Penny can reduce these pay-offs by giving slightly more attention through eye contact to the bored and hostile-looking people, than she gives to the smilers. This will go against her natural inclination, but when she makes steady eye contact with her detractors, she shows them that she is prepared to engage in direct and equal communication with them. She shows them that she is not frightened of them. She deprives them of the pay-offs they get from literally seeing 'the whites of her eyes'. So it can be tactically effective to give difficult people plenty of attention through eye contact. It buys into their need to have their self-importance acknowledged and to appease the small child inside them who's shouting, 'me, me, me!'

Panel interviews favour the more outwardly-confident candidates. One reason for this is that these candidates are more likely to make eye contact with the whole panel as they speak, rather than homing in on the individual who's asked the question. As they give the answer, starting off directing it to the questioner, and then including the whole panel in their eye contact, they influence all the people present. This tip applies to meetings and presentations too: when making a point or answering a question, include everyone present in your scanning. In that way you will ensure keeping everyone's attention. When just making eye contact with one person, we start to exclude everyone else and set up a private conversation. Confidence is about appearing comfortable influencing everyone present.

CONFIDENCE TRICK: The Eyes Have It

- Work on developing the steady gaze, which moves comfortably around groups of people. Check that you make as much eye contact when you are *speaking* as when you are listening to others. Self-effacing people are often very attentive as listeners, but do not make so much eye contact when they themselves are the objects of attention. And perhaps not surprisingly, generally, women make more sustained eye contact when they listen and men make more sustained eye contact when they speak . . .

- If you're talking to someone who obviously has difficulty in making eye contact themselves, then staring at them with a penetrating gaze is going to emphasise the difference between your communicating styles, rather than making you more harmonious. Gaze at them steadily and gently, and then look away. Then gaze again and so on. Through doing this we can actually let people know that it is safe and comfortable for them to make eye contact with us.

- One of the keys to John Kennedy's charismatic communicating style, was the way he made eye contact. When we look at other people we tend to focus on one eye. Kennedy apparently, as he looked at others made searching eye contact, shifting his focus from one eye to the other. This technique gives the impression of soul-searching, of really wanting to know what makes the other person tick. Try it.

- Sometimes, we avoid making eye contact with others because we find them irresistibly attractive. We don't want them to see our pupils dilating uncontrollably. So, next time someone seems to be avoiding your gaze in a meeting – that *could* be the reason why!

And now on to another important aspect of non-verbal confidence, so important that it warrants its own chapter: clothes and appearance signals.

12 *Looking Confident*

CONFIDENCE KEY: Clothes, accessories, grooming

THERE'S an argument to be made, I suppose, that if you are really confident you needn't give a jot about your appearance. But then we overlook the fact that confidence is often about matching our own ideas about ourselves against reality. In reality, other people often judge us according to how we look. And many of us want to present versions of ourselves that are appropriate, say, for the business world, or the charity sector, or public life. In caring about our appearance, we also show consideration for other people's sense of aesthetics. We consider, for instance, the pain to their eyes before we put on that luminous orange suit we're so fond of.

Sometimes our fantasies determine the way we dress. Like the man in the Rolex, red braces, sharp pin-striped suit and slicked back hair, who fancies himself as Gordon Gekko – the Michael Douglas role in the movie *Wall Street* – and wears that fantasy into work. Quite often, our fantasies are more fun if we keep them to ourselves or share them with a small number of people – in private.

Our clothes can also suggest to others that we want to be very different from who we are, that we are not happy with ourselves. For instance, the middle-aged woman who dresses like a young romantic heroine of a Barbara Cartland novel, with long fluffy hair and flouncy dresses and then wonders why people seem slightly confused about how to respond to her in the office. She'd be wiser dressing in her fantasies at home and in her social life, and wearing something more businesslike for working hours – perhaps a tailored dress and jacket.

There is no doubt, however, that *appropriate* dress, reflecting our own, individual taste and suitability for the occasion, can help us project confidence. Through wearing clothes in which we look and feel comfortable and which suit us – drawing attention to our best features – we can say to the world, 'I enjoy being who I am.' Never mind that the raw material we have to work with is hardly Cindy Crawford or Richard Gere standard. We've demonstrated the self-esteem necessary to have thought out how best to present ourselves. And we have worked out *our own* rules, applied them, and are now getting on with life. Giving some thought and time to how we look is an investment that saves on both in the long term. Once we have worked out what suits us, we won't need to think about clothes very often, and we will avoid costly mistakes. Confident people are not constantly worrying about how they look; they're too busy getting on with *doing* things.

Free, Easy and Fun

In line with my own thinking, ease and freedom have become important themes in fashion. It is very noticeable how ideas about what is appropriate have changed, since the late 1980s. The rules about what people should and shouldn't wear have got looser. More and more women wear trousers or leggings to work while some men choose to wear sports or casual jackets and trousers, with coloured shirts and ties rather than pin-striped suits.

Of course, it depends what you do and where you work: the city, finance and legal sectors often still follow quite traditional rules – while retail businesses, the media, health and the public sectors have become a lot more relaxed. In my opinion, this freeing-up of clothes rules is a welcome change and gives us greater opportunity to express our individuality and creativity through how we look. Uniform detracts from self-expression.

This greater freedom for self-expression means that clothes for work, as well as play, can be fun. The recession has forced many upmarket designers to produce cheaper, good quality ranges of clothes and there is a vast selection available to suit most pockets. There is enormous satisfaction, as well as confidence, to be gained from knowing that what you are wearing suits you in terms of your personality, your shape and your colouring. You can express your sensual appreciation and enjoyment of the most valuable of assets – yourself.

In this chapter, we are going to look at how projecting confidence through our clothes can be made easy. We will consider: choosing clothes, how to feel comfortable, whether confidence need be costly, and how grooming and accessories can convey confidence.

Suiting Ourselves

In Chapter Three, I talked about role-playing. This is a useful idea to reconsider when we talk about appearance, because, to play a role effectively, we have to get our costume right. It's especially relevant to think in terms of role expectations: how do *we* expect to play our roles and what do *others* expect of us in those roles?

Donna has recently started working as an advertising account manager. She likes working in advertising, and the way her colleagues tend to dress in a casual but fashionable way. This suits Donna, who likes to keep her wardrobe absolutely up to the moment. When she first started her job, however, she overlooked differences between what was accepted in the office, and what her clients expected. At a meeting with a client from a bank, she turned up in a grungey outfit of smock and leggings. Although the meeting went quite well, afterwards the client mentioned to Donna's boss that he had reservations about Donna's youth and ability to handle the account. She sensibly realised that her appearance had, to a great extent, contributed to this impression. Donna decided to invest in a 'conservative client's' outfit – one that would give her appearance the gravitas and credibility needed.

Women are still judged more by their appearance than men are, and though we have far greater choice – with a wide range of different shapes and designs to choose from – we also have greater scope to get it wrong. The guidelines I'm going to talk about in this chapter are for both sexes, but in some sections I will be making specific separate points for women and men.

Back to role: when people make mistakes in their choice of clothes, they have often not considered the role they are playing. For example, the university student who still dresses like an undergraduate in the blue-chip corporation that's just employed him, or the woman returning to work who dresses for the school run, rather than the board room, or the expert who goes on television dressed to shock rather than to convey authority and credibility. We need to be aware of the qualities that we want to project in our various roles, and how our dress sense can help us to do this.

CONFIDENCE TRICK: A Fitting Role

- To find out whether your wardrobe is adaptable and accept-able for the roles you play, first of all write down the most important roles you play and the qualities you like to project through these roles. These qualities will act as guidelines for your clothing decisions. Stuck for words? Then here are some ideas for qualities you might want to consider: warmth, coolness, efficiency, creativity, organ-ised, flexible, powerful, generous, authoritative, rural, urban, businesslike, intellectual, arty, relaxed, effective, wealthy, spiritual, alternative, mainstream, conventional, rebellious, serious, youthful, rock and roll, responsible, stimulating, dramatic, outgoing, introspective.

- You may find it helpful to think of someone who you feel dresses well and appropriately. What qualities does their style of dressing convey about their role?

- Think about the time you spend playing each of, say, your three most important roles. Work these out as percentages. That is, say, you could spend 60 per cent of your week as a consultant, 35 per cent of your week as a husband and a father, and 5 per cent as a sports enthusiast.

- Now set these percentages against the clothes you have in your wardrobe. Does the balance in your wardrobe reflect how you spend your time in your different roles?

- If there's an imbalance, resolve to supplement and whittle down, as required.

Raw Material

To suit yourself and to project confidence, you need to make a quick assessment of your raw material: your shape, your size and scale, your colouring and texture of your hair and skin. These will determine the

177

appropriate cut of clothes, the cloth – in terms of colour and texture – and the type of accessories you should choose.

Shaping up

Most of us have a good idea about our shape – and how we would like it to be different. But throughout this chapter, I'd like you to think about how you are *at the current time*, rather than how you would like to be as a perfect, fantasy figure. Your height will need to be considered, relative to your girth. Are you round or square shouldered? Do you have large shoulders compared to the rest of you? Is your waist thick or slender? How large are your hips relative to the rest of your body? Do you have long or short legs? What do you consider to be good features about your body? And which ones would you rather make less of?

We should dress to flatter, rather than to fight our shapes. So if we have features that we dislike – like a thick waist, large stomach or big hips – then we should choose clothes shapes that skim loosely and without detail over these areas. If we are statuesque, tall and expansive, then we can carry off contrasting tops and bottoms more effectively than if we are small. Double-breasted suits which 'break up' the body twice as much as single-breasted ones will look good. We can carry off larger patterns and flowing garments better than our smaller colleagues. If large and weighty, we should dress to convey substance, wearing generously cut clothes in natural fabrics that breathe well and move easily with the body.

If small and wide, we need to streamline ourselves by the cut of our clothes. We should avoid unnecessary seams, pockets, belts and ruffles, and go for simple lines. We can add vibrancy through our choice of jewellery and ties. Tops, bottoms, tights and shoes all in shades of one colour will help small women to look more streamlined, while vertical stripes and single-breasted suits will streamline small, chunky men. Small and slight, we can wear neat-fitting garments, that do not overpower us. We can wear more detail than our plumper friends, but need to keep patterns, pockets and buttons on the small side. Heavily textured fabrics such as tweed will overpower us; we'll be better off choosing a fine wool or gabardine.

Soft and sharp

When you look at yourself in a mirror, do you see lots of curvy lines? Or do you look angular? Though women are, of course, curvier than men, some of us are much more angular than others: with square shoulders, flattish chests, thickish waists and comparatively slim hips. We can choose to emphasise or play down our curves or angularity through the cut of our clothes. Just think of jacket lapels and hemlines: they can be curved and rounded, or sharp and angular. Where we need to be careful, is when our bodies are markedly curvy or angular: dressing to the other extreme may make us look uncomfortable with our shapes. The boyishly shaped woman, for instance, who drapes herself in flounces and frills, or the well-padded man who girds himself in stiff, tight tailoring will both look ill at ease with themselves.

This 'soft' and 'sharp' distinction can also be applied to fabrics – a suede skirt or trousers, for instance, will be much softer than the same garment in gabardine. We can extend this discrimination to all sorts of garments: a round-necked, lacy-knit cotton sweater is going to be a much 'curvier' garment than a fine lambswool V-necked sweater with neat shoulder seams. If confidence for you is about friendliness and approachability, then you could accentuate this through the first option: on the other hand, if you prefer to interpret confidence as being about structure and control, you could accentuate this through the second.

Colour cues

Colour choices will also matter. A few years ago, I wrote a bestselling book called *Your Total Image* detailing advice on how to make a good impression through behaviour and appearance. At that time, clothes were not part of my special area of expertise and when I started appearing in newspapers and on television, several people offered me advice on how I should dress.

I was rather sceptical about this form of 'image consultancy' and being told what to wear. Like a lot of women of my generation, black was my preferred choice – for everything. Being told that I should wear 'teal' and 'apricot' made me feel dubious. I ignored the advice, and continued to dress in my 'creative' mainly black, slightly rebellious style.

More recently, though, I met a woman called Irene Nathan, who I thought treated the whole subject of dressing in a different way. Rather than applying rigid rules to clothes, she has a real skill for rapidly identifying what people should accentuate, in order to enjoy how they look. I went shopping with Irene, and in almost every shop we visited she found something she thought suited me, that I would never have chosen myself. And she proved to be right.

Now I spend very little time and not that much money on clothes. Irene suggested I choose deep rich colours and plain shapes, with predominantly gold jewellery. The frequent packing I need to do for business trips is always easy, because the range of colours Irene suggested all go together. And, luckily for me, I continue to receive her ideas because, on our confidence courses, she passes on her excellent advice to others.

Here are some of her guidelines you might like to use:

Undertone colouring

Whatever our racial origins, as individuals we tend to have a dominance of either blue or yellow undertones in our colouring. Typical English rose colouring, with ash-blonde hair, pink and white skin and blue eyes, for instance, will have blue undertones dominating. Celtic colouring, of reddish hair, freckles on creamy skin, and green or brown eyes will show more yellow. Look at your skin colour, natural hair shade and eye colour, and decide whether you lean towards blue or yellow. A quick way of helping you decide can be to hold a bluey white up against your face, and then a cream, and to see which suits you best.

Many people instinctively choose clothes in colours which suit them, anyway. However, once you've consciously identified whether you can lean towards warm or cool undertones, it can be very useful in helping you to choose the main colours in your wardrobe. This is because colours come in many different shades. Take red for instance, which you might be wearing in a blouse or tie. Some reds look quite orangey and have a lot of yellow undertones: others have a lot more blue in them and veer towards crimson. You will look best in the shade that accentuates your natural undertones.

Emotional responses

Colours work in a powerful way on our subconscious responses. For example, when we see a red traffic light we rarely consciously think: red means danger, so I must stop. We are just conditioned to see that colour light and respond very quickly. And we can't always predict or control other people's responses to the colours we wear. For example, if you are meeting someone you wish to impress and to do this you go for a canary coloured jacket which you think will make you memorable, you can't predict that they observe a rule that 'people shouldn't dress to draw attention to themselves'.

A quick game of colour association when you buy clothes, can work wonders. For instance, grey/brown/navy may get you responding with, 'safe', 'reliable', 'authoritative', all of which could be appropriate for what you want to convey at work, on a day-to-day basis. Whereas, red/turquoise/green may get you responding with 'dynamic', 'calming', and 'growth oriented', respectively – any of which may be feelings that you want to stimulate in your clients and customers.

Wearing darker colours will undoubtedly help you to be taken seriously, but this doesn't mean that you have to merge into the sea of navy and grey that make up most business environments. An almost black, charcoal, bitter chocolate, deep burgundy or dark green all make interesting and sophisticated alternatives.

Drama and subtlety

Through the colours we wear and put together, we can choose to emphasise the drama or subtlety of our colouring. It's useful to ask yourself: How much contrast is there between my skin, hair and eye colour and how much similarity? With black hair, blue eyes and pale skin, the contrast will be marked, and you can accentuate this through sharp contrasts in colour – black or navy and white, for instance. With sandy hair, freckles and hazel eyes, similarity of colouring will be much more evident, and this can be reinforced by dressing in complementary shades of olive green, tan and cream.

Texture guidelines

Another aspect that image consultants look for is texture. With silky hair, fine skin and bright blue or green eyes, your appearance is likely to shine, rather than smoulder. With coarser hair, thicker skin and deep brown or grey eyes, then your appearance is likely to suggest muted depth rather than brightness. We can choose clothes and accessories that emphasise these qualities: enhancing shine and brightness through smooth silks and leathers and shiny metals and stones, or enhancing muted depth through more textured wool, suede and matt metals.

Hair colour

A few years ago, I read an American dress-for-success book in which the author suggested that, if you wanted to look really 'together', you should keep your hair close to its natural colour and follow through this colour when buying big items of clothing and accessories. At the time, again, I thought this advice was doubtful, but I started to notice that Japanese people, with their smooth, shining black hair, also look terrific in black clothes. Clearly, too, redheads look good in tan or rust suede and leather coats and accessories. So, if you want to simplify the range of colours you choose, and to always look co-ordinated, head to toe, restrict yourself to colours that echo your hair colouring, when choosing main items and accessories.

Size-right accessories

Accessories should also be chosen with size and scale in mind. A small, delicate-boned person will be dwarfed by a large, bulky briefcase and chunky divers' watch. On the other hand, a big-boned person of substance will look incongruous with a slim, streamlined briefcase and a dainty watch. Match the scale of jewellery and accessories to your size, and be aware that you can accentuate curves or angles too, through the shapes and patterns you choose.

Convenience Confidence

Some people are very interested in fashion and their appearance. You may be one of these lucky types who enjoy thinking about and shopping for clothes. I've a colleague like this. She plans her wardrobe with military precision and always looks immaculate. But those of us who find it all rather an effort, need to establish rules or guidelines for ourselves to make it easier:

- Image consultants can provide personalised guidelines, for both men and women. Find one via recommendation, perhaps from someone you think always looks good. Failing such advice, you will find addresses of companies who provide this service in the information section at the back of this book. Seeking professional advice is a good way to get a fresh viewpoint about your appearance, and to save yourself time and money.

- Anything you have hanging in your wardrobe that you haven't worn for two years, could be doing more good in a charity shop.

- Though it sounds limiting, if you do restrict yourself to certain shapes and predominant colours in your wardrobe, you will find that items work better together. For instance, as a woman with a thickish waist you might prefer leggings and long sweaters and tops for leisurewear, and team the same leggings with long jackets for work. When all these clothes are, for example, in rich autumnal colours that suit your colouring, you will find that a good quality pair of tan shoes or boots and a tan bag go with almost everything you wear.

Men's clothing choices have traditionally been more restricted than those of women – but they have improved significantly in recent years. Even so, if you prefer to make dressing really simple and convenient, choose a colour and style that suits you, and repeat it several times throughout your wardrobe. A charcoal, single-breasted jacket, for example, could come in linen, wool and tweed.

This is the way many celebrities make their appearances distinctive and memorable. Jean Muir, the clothes designer, only ever wears navy. Richard Branson almost always wears his uniform of sweater and jeans. Jennifer Saunders is often to be seen wearing clothes from the designer Betty Jackson, while Dawn French wears gorgeous clothes from her own range. Jonathan Ross is always nattily attired in sharp, designer suits.

- Buy clothes that don't require a lot of ironing. These days, many low-maintenance synthetic fabrics look good and feel comfortable to wear.

- Have one utterly conventional outfit that you know you can wear when in doubt. The navy and white polka dot or small print dress with a navy jacket is a good one for women; for men a navy suit is acceptable anywhere. Navy tends to suit more people than black. On some of us – especially the pale skinned – black can look very draining. People with stronger colouring – like the Japanese, for example – look particularly striking in black.

- Remember that colour is very evocative. While a rich dark brown can look sophisticated and set off brunette or red hair beautifully, it is more of a rustic colour than an urban one. As a woman in a bright red jacket or a man in a bright red tie, you will look as though you want to attract attention – and you will do just that. Remember: bright, warm colours 'advance' on the eye, while cold, muted ones 'retreat'.

At the time of writing, bright colours are less fashionable. Something to do with the 'softer' mood of the 1990s, compared with the brasher 1980s, I think. Bright colours can also overpower the wearer, so that people see the garment rather than the person. This isn't dressing with confidence. Bear in mind, too, that bold, vibrant colours which look wonderful in a warm climate, often look harsh in greyish British light.

Comfortably confident

People who look confident always look comfortable in what they are wearing. They don't look as though they're trying hard to create an impression, or as though they have spent hours getting ready. The secret of feeling and looking comfortable lies in choosing clothes that fit well, and are made in easy-to-wear, easy-care fabrics.

We expect to buy ready-to-wear clothes that will fit us perfectly, but this is quite a demand when you think of the many different shapes and sizes, human beings come in. Fortunately, and relatively recently, manufacturers have cottoned on to this and chains like Marks and Spencer offer clothes in a wide variety of sizes and lengths. And many shops will carry out alterations when necessary, though most charge extra for this service.

It's always wiser, too, to buy clothes cut on the generous side. It can be very tempting, if you intend to lose weight and fall in love with a garment, to buy it hoping that it will fit you in six months time. The trouble is, you can't be sure that you *will* lose the weight or *if* you do, where exactly you will lose it from. We feel and look comfortable in our clothes when we can move easily in them, without buttons or material straining. They will also last longer.

Any aspect of a garment that causes it to be stiff: such as being made of thick material like a tweed; or causes it to hang unnaturally over the body: because of big shoulder pads, for example, will make you look and feel uncomfortable. Soft and fine fabrics, such as cottons, silks and wools, and a cut that allows the garment to move with the body, will convey ease – and confidence.

The cost of confidence

The cost per wear theory is that if you buy a garment that costs £100 and wear it two hundred times, then its cost is fifty pence a wearing. On the other hand, if you buy an item for £10 and wear it only once, then it has cost that price to wear. We recoup our investment by how often we use the item.

The trouble is, we might get bored with a garment that we wear two hundred times. In my experience, apart from one expensive and adored leather coat, my favourite clothes that I wear time and time again are cosy old sweaters and track suit trousers. So while 'investment' dressing, that is, buying a few expensive, classic items that we can wear time and time again, makes good common sense, it's not much fun. You might prefer to buy quite a lot of clothes two or three times a year; buying from the high street or designer diffusion ranges – cheaper, mass-market versions of top designs, which are now proliferating.

If you want to look expensive, you don't necessarily have to wear expensive clothes. Wearing colours that occur in nature: neutrals and naturals, are a good start. Garish colours can look cheap. Wear simply cut clothes; the fewer the seams, the less the quality of the stitching matters. As the weather in Britain rarely goes to extremes, buy most of your clothes in middle-weight material. Unless you travel abroad a great deal, you're unlikely to get much wear out of heavyweight coats or sleeveless, light tops. Choose modern classics like the linen jacket and the three-button, fine wool sweater. Buy thirtysomething liberal and modern, rather than Wall Street conservative and traditional. Add interest by wearing distinctive jewellery and good quality accessories.

Confidence constants

We're talking about regular routines here, starting at the top with your hair. This is a most important feature through which you can convey confidence. A well-shaped, well-maintained hairstyle that suits your face is an asset to your appearance and one that you wear every day.

Looking confident is about hair that frames your face in a flattering way, rather than a floppy fringe behind which you hide. As we get older, a shorter cut which lets other people see our features clearly and attracts the observer's eye upwards, rather than accentuating the downward pull of gravity which accompanies ageing, often looks more confident. Again, find a good hairdresser through recommendation. And remember, a good hairdresser is one who will cut and style your hair to suit your face and your hair texture – not simply give you the 'trendy' style of the moment.

Other aspects of grooming also help the appearance of confidence. Well shaped, defined eyebrows (they, and eyelashes, can be dyed) draw attention to the eyes, and make other features look stronger. Also, nourish your skin from within by eating a sensible diet as well as by applying moisturisers, to keep it smooth, soft and blemish free.

Women can also use make up skilfully to enhance their best features and play down less perfect ones. A make-up lesson, from a specialist teaching centre or from a department store cosmetician can be a good investment, if you are unsure about how to apply make-up to best advantage.

For both sexes, confidence killers like poor teeth, dandruff, bad breath, heavy perspiration can all be treated nowadays. So don't endure them.

Also, indulge yourself in expressing confidence through frequently used accessories. Spend time and money on choosing important items like watches and workbags or briefcases. You are likely to use them every day, and they will give you more pleasure than any single item of clothing would. In some businesses, people notice watches and bags far more than they do garments, because they have become big status symbols.

Enjoy having beautiful objects to enhance your appearance and express your aesthetic sense, good taste and sensuality. Show that you care for yourself on the outside as well as the inside – and you will exude confidence and self-esteem.

CONFIDENCE TRICK: Clothing Inventory

Answering the following questions will help you to be much more confident about your clothing and accessory choices in the future. Keep your answers for reference when you go shopping.

- Looking at your size and shape, what are the best features you wish to accentuate, and what would you like to play down?

- Are you best suited to sharp tailoring, stiff fabrics, or curvier lines and soft fabrics? Or some sort of compromise between the two?

- How would you describe your colouring? Predominantly with warm or cool undertones? Is there much contrast between the shades of your hair, skin and eyes, or are they fairly complementary?

- Are your features bright and shiny, or are they more muted and deep? What texture is your skin and hair? Can you accentuate these aspects through your choice of fabric?

- Can you accentuate your hair colouring through having a significant part of your wardrobe and accessories in a certain shade?

- What size accessories suit your size and scale?

- If you had an ideal uniform – in terms of shape, colour and fabric – what would it be? Are you able to reflect this more through your choice of clothes?

- If you don't have one, can you buy yourself an accessory that you really like and will use every day? Spend more than you might do normally, if necessary, and imbue this gift to yourself with significance. It will symbolise that you have the self-esteem to be kind to yourself and to treat yourself. Remember this every time you look at this item and it will act as a confidence anchor.

13 *Projecting Professionalism*

CONFIDENCE KEY: What professionalism is, behaving professionally in various situations, charisma

---

PROFESSIONALISM means appearing competent, calm and controlled at work; if you like, it is a type of advanced confidence. And if you want other people to know about your professionalism then you have to embark on a conscious self-promotion campaign, as Keith discovered. He is a finance director:

'I'm a quiet person, not very good at blowing my own trumpet: it simply wasn't done in our family. In my first job, which lasted for about five years, I became incredibly frustrated. I was good at my work, but was passed over for promotion a couple of times, in favour of two more outgoing but not very competent colleagues. It just got too much and I was about to leave the company, when my manager took me aside and gave me a pep talk. He told me that I was achieving a great deal on the job, but other people were taking the credit. He advised me to ensure that all my ideas and projects were "copyrighted" as mine – that officially and unofficially people knew of my involvement. This advice turned my career round.'

When we are heavily involved with a project, many of us make the mistake of thinking that other people will automatically know what we're up to. This is not the case, of course: doing your work well and letting people know you are doing your work well are two separate activities. Very confident people have no problem in running their own mini PR campaigns on the subject of themselves.

And the extent to which others respond to the publicity is truly amazing. Take the actress Demi Moore for instance (she's also known as 'Gimme' Moore). Described by many as a modest talent, Demi

Moore now commands amongst the highest fees in Hollywood. For several years, she has played the off-screen role of a prima donna, being difficult and demanding. She has instructed people how to respond to her, and they are following her instructions. And this doesn't just happen in the rarefied world of Hollywood. Social psychology reports many experiments which show that the majority of us are extremely susceptible to suggestion. This is especially so when those suggestions come from figures of authority, people we look up to, or from members of our own peer group.

However, while Demi clearly doesn't have any self-doubts, many of us wouldn't feel comfortable running publicity campaigns which suggest we are brilliant, when secretly inside we suspect we are not. We would like to believe in our own ability *first*, and *then* work on projecting it to others. So let's get started . . .

What is Professionalism?

In the narrowest sense, according to Sandra Dawson in her book *Analysing Organisations*, professionalism is to do with:

- Commitment to a distinct body of knowledge.

- Specific and lengthy training.

- Restrictive entry.

- Prescribed codes of ethics and standards of behaviour.

- Proclaimed concern for client groups.

- Peer group evaluation, control and promotion.

For organisations, professionals can pose problems. They can regard their professional status as taking priority over membership of the organisation. So presenting a paper at a professional conference will be regarded as more important than finishing a project for the organisation. Our identity as a 'doctor', 'solicitor', 'teacher', 'engineer' or 'manager' may become more significant to us than who we work for. Increasingly, so the management gurus predict, organisations will have to learn how to work effectively with floating pools of such professionals, rather than company women and men.

But, for our purpose, I use professionalism in a looser sense, to mean credibility and competence. I look at what professionalism means and how to get a reputation for it with others. I look at how we can convey professionalism in interviews (job and media), meetings and presentations. And I investigate a quality that people on courses are always telling me that they want to understand and acquire – the quality of charisma.

Increasingly in the future, it will be essential to appear professional. According to management guru Charles Handy, we are no longer going to have 'jobs for life'. Indeed, the effects of the recession have already meant that careers like banking, which used to offer lifetime security, no longer do so. Handy says that in the future the norm will be to have ten or twelve different jobs and two or three different careers. We will be 'portfolio' workers, needing to be able to cope with frequent change and to be as adaptable as possible. One of the best resources we can use to help us with this is confidence in our own professionalism, so let's look at ways of achieving this happy position. There are three main areas we can look at: learning as a professional, communicating as a professional, and having a keen sense of timing.

Learning as a Pro

Professionals keep on learning, not simply to keep up to date, but to get ahead. The wage gap between graduates and those who didn't go to university is widening. And because there are so many graduates with first degrees seeking employment, second degrees distinguish the exceptional job candidate from the average.

But learning is not just about formal mainstream education: it's about acquiring a range of skills, 'sampling' other subjects in evening classes and workshops, and chasing your dreams. One of the best decisions I made in my life was to go back to full-time education for a year at the age of twenty-eight. I was chasing a dream. I had always wanted to go to drama school, but had instead gone to university to do an academic rather than a practical study of the subject. My year's study at a drama school – to get an advanced diploma in voice studies – resulted in a change of career and the birth of my training company.

Formal and professional qualifications look good on a cv, build self-confidence and provide potential employers with tangible evidence of your abilities. Learn for life.

To project your professionalism, you need to show other people that you have expert power and information power. Expert power is to do with knowledge about your subject; information power is to do with knowing all the latest developments in your field, and who's who at the top. Expert power is acquired and exchanged through specialist journals, trade papers, conferences, and professional associations and institutes. Information power is exchanged through print again, and also through conversation, formal and informal – often referred to as 'networking'.

The best source of learning for all of us is other people, so associate with people who you respect and who you can learn from. But don't take identification with your role models too far: you can never *be* another person although you can learn from observing what it is they *do*. You don't want to end up suffering from what the Germans call *geltungsbedurfnis* (try saying that with a mouthful of pistachios), which means having so little self-worth that you absorb glamour from others. We learn from others when we study process – what the person does and how they do it – rather than being preoccupied with effect.

Communicating as a Pro

Present yourself as a professional. See previous chapters. This is as important for men as women, perhaps even more so. Social conditioning has meant that women are more used to being judged on the basis of their self-presentation; many men have big gaps in this aspect of their education.

Professionalism is about awareness and sensitivity. It involves concern for what your peers think about your work, and for recognition from them. This means building relationships with your peers so that you are in a position to encourage their feedback. Ask them whether they would be prepared to give you constructive feedback, and whether they would like it from you in return.

Professionalism also involves concern for client and customer welfare, not least when dealing with difficult people: the cynical, the hostile and the self-important. What transactional analysis calls 'positive strokes' are vital when handling people who don't feel good about themselves, or others. (And self-doubt often underlies difficult behaviour.)

Bear in mind too, that we influence others most effectively and in a long-lasting way by getting them involved. Peers, subordinates and superiors will become more committed to your ideas if you ask them to consider your proposals and give their opinions. When we're truly confident, we should also feel comfortable with suggesting possibilities that are unlikely to be realised but that generate new ideas from others.

Because many of us have been brought up to be self-effacing, we need also to take a strategic approach to self-promotion – communicating our worth to others. We should be able to match our achievements and highspots to the listener, for which purpose it's useful to have in your mind a computer-like list of what you've achieved and what you've really enjoyed. These items are then ready to be selected and mentioned when useful and appropriate; update them regularly.

As well as fine-tuning our own testimony in this manner, it's worth accumulating tangible evidence of our worth. Store and use everything that others might interpret as proof of your credibility: certificates, thank-you letters, testimonials, positive evaluations and press cuttings. Keep a file that you can bring out when necessary. If people phone you to commend or thank you for something you've done especially well, accept the gesture graciously. Where appropriate, ask them whether you might use their recommendation in the future.

We will feel more comfortable drawing attention to ourselves when we use methods that suit us, as individuals. A colleague of mine was very dubious about the value of networking. So she decided to try it for six months and to use it to raise her profile. Every time she went to a meeting, lunch or talk she would ask a question, often of a humorous nature. Very soon, people started phoning the office to ask if my colleague was coming to events. Just by contributing in a positive, memorable way, she got herself noticed and in demand.

Some people, however, have unrealistic ideas about networking. They expect people to want to help them without giving anything back. We need to remember that networking is about *exchange* and to acknowledge this openly in our dealings with one another. We can avoid misunderstanding through mentioning this directly: 'In doing this, can I call upon you for a favour in the future?' Or, 'Thanks very much for your help. I'll return the favour when I get an opportunity.'

Let people who can help you know what you want and where your ambitions lie. Other people can't mind read your goals. Overcome embarrassment by conveying them in a spirit of enthusiasm: 'Something I'd really like to do is . . .' As well as enabling you to get advice and encouragement for your ambitions, you are more likely to achieve them when they are stated aloud. The act of announcing your ambitions fixes them more clearly as goals. Also, once other people know about them, achieving our ambitions involves gaining recognition – and avoiding losing face. That does not mean, however, that you are not free to change your plans at any stage. Never pursue a goal simply to meet other people's expectations.

But what if you don't like socialising and dread the idea of using it to further your career? Then develop your writing skills, become an expert in a specific area and write articles and letters for journals and magazines. Express controversial opinions to get attention.

In writing and speaking, try to interact with people in a relaxed manner. This is the style of business in the 1990s, with relationships given as much emphasis as the task in hand.

Timing as a Pro

Professionals show respect for their own time and other people's, especially if they are charging by the hour. When we're constantly late for meetings, the message we give other people is that our time is more valuable than theirs. This can be insulting, and it won't make others well-disposed towards us. (Incidentally, there is a joke that a psychoanalyst will interpret time accordingly: if you're late for your appointment, then it indicates that you're aggressive; if you're on time for your appointment, then it indicates that you're obsessive; if you're early for your appointment, then it indicates that you're anxious. No way to win here.)

We can extend respect for people's time to phone calls, as well. If we need to discuss a matter at length, then it's considerate and conducive to a happy result to ask at the outset whether you've called at an appropriate time.

Specific Situations: Interviews

At Voiceworks, we often work for outplacement companies who help senior executives to change jobs. Often, these executives have recently been made redundant, and are in a state of shock at having to face job interviews. Some succumb to despair: but the majority regard coaching on communication and presentation as an unexpected opportunity to acquire new skills. Those who approach interviews with professionalism do the following:

- They keep up-to-date with news concerning the relevant business or organisation. They research company reports, trade papers, and business pages of the national newspapers, and they ask contacts for information. This gives them an opportunity to show how informed they are at the interview.

- They regard the interview as a process, as much as an event resulting in an outcome: As well as having a clear purpose, they will realise there is great value in what happens *during* the interview. Apart from job opportunities, interviews allow scope for making contacts – with the interviewers and other interviewees. In this manner they find out about the particular company and the image it wishes to present, create a good impression even though they may not be right for the job in question; and they hone their interview skills.

- They are comfortable about boasting. Those of us who have been conditioned to be modest need to practise, so that we get comfortable listing our most relevant achievements. We can't assume that the interviewers have scrutinised our cvs in detail. Our words need to spell out explicitly how what we've achieved in the past, matches the employer's present and future needs. We can use humour and a manner that suggests we don't take ourselves *too* seriously – but the message that we are appropriately qualified and motivated must come through. If really necessary, announce your discomfort with a 'It's not usual for me to promote myself in this way, but . . .'

- They handle difficult questions effectively. Some insecure people use the role of interviewer as a form of exorcism during which they hit the candidates with all their own inadequacies. Don't let such tactics unnerve you. Preserve your self-possession with, 'I'm happy to answer all your questions, but I'm curious about why you should ask that one?' Needless to say, this needs to be delivered in a respectful, open way.

Going on the Box

With the vast expansion in the number of radio and television channels, producers and researchers are hungry for news items to fill the airwaves. If you enjoy a fairly high profile among your peers, you may decide this is the time to widen your audience and go public. It is best to start off on local radio and regional or day-time television, where learning need not be too costly or damaging ... Decide which programmes your knowledge would be relevant for and call the programme office to find out whether it is a producer, editor or researcher you should be contacting. Then send a letter and your cv, indicating your area of expertise. Quite a few programme organisers have database files of experts to call up as appropriate.

On both radio and television, mastering the sound-bite delivery is all about thinking about who your audience is, in terms of content. For instance, an audience for the eleven o'clock show in the morning, will have different interests from the audience for the six-thirty business programme in the evening. To ensure that you are relevant to your audience, always ask the programme staff how they define a typical audience member. Find out what role you are expected to play: 'concerned public sector manager', 'greedy capitalist', 'unfortunate victim', and 'successful role model' are typical. Be meticulous about your appearance, relax your face and body beforehand (see exercises in Chapter Eleven), and rehearse what you want to say, aloud, using short sentences. Remember that the interviewer is there as an intermediary between you and the listeners or viewers. If you respond to her or him with a constructive and helpful attitude, then your audience will judge you accordingly.

Group-Meetings and Presentations

As more and more organisations get flatter in their structures, with less hierarchy and fewer layers of managers, so the need for meetings increases. The 'cascade' style of management, in which vision and direction stream through the organisation, is all the rage at the time of writing. It involves plenty of clear communication: up, down and across the layers.

But in many workplaces, meetings often lack this clear purpose. Use your time effectively and only attend if there are items on the agenda that are relevant to you. You can wield power most effectively by determining the agenda. So, if you want to take a Machiavellian approach, work on the person whose role it is to create the agenda. Put your items in early, and if you suspect agreement on your proposals is going to be hard-won, then the best slot for them is immediately after a suggestion that is likely to be completely quashed. By comparison then, what you are proposing may not sound so extreme.

Sit next to people who are likely to be your supporters, and where the chairperson can clearly see you. Speak early on in the meeting, and when you speak be sure to include everyone in your gaze and attention.

Make sure that you are given credit for your ideas in the minutes. Don't let some smooth-talking operator hijack your laurels. Always have the last word on any ideas you have introduced – if necessary checking with the minute-taker that this last word has been noted: 'So we're agreed to act on my idea for disbanding the typing pool ... Mark, have you put that down?' Be aware that the most effective way of influencing logically is to put your reason first: 'As everyone in this organisation does their own word-processing now,' and then your proposal, 'I'd like to suggest we disband the typing pool.' This is a better way of putting it than vice-versa: in which event the proposal can create such a strong response in others that they do not wait to hear your reasons.

Again for the Machiavellians: if you offer people several choices when you suggest something, you are likely to encounter less resistance than if you say there is one definitive route that must be followed. If you want to conceal which choice you really want to push, then put it at the end of the list rather than at the beginning.

In presenting to groups, professional skills are about entertaining people as well as giving them information. Visuals should look impressive and humour can be used to connect with and relax the audience. The best presenters find a definite style of presenting that suits them *as individuals.* Jan took a while to work this out:

Jan is a computer specialist in a large telecommunications company. A graduate recruit, she has to present to people who are a lot older and more senior than she is and though this never phased her, she did notice that her presentations varied widely in quality. When she analysed this, she realised that her presentations went down well when she spoke with conviction and passion. When these qualities were absent, however, her presentations were dull, over-correct affairs. She resolved always to think carefully about how to angle the subject, so that she could make all her presentations express her beliefs and convictions, while still conveying the facts and evidence necessary to present a logical case. Jan has gone on to build an excellent reputation as a presenter, which has helped her to gain early promotion.

Professional presenters are as skilled and comfortable with holding the floor as they are with taking questions. And they can switch effortlessly from taking the initiative to reacting. Going back to the technique described in Chapter Nine, good presenters are able to move into 'a member of the audience's position', and to move into the 'detached observer' position, where they control tricky events through commenting on them: 'That's a difficult question, I'll need a moment to think about that', 'As it's five minutes before the bar opens, I think I'll call it a day. Thank you very much for listening.'

Confidence and Charisma

What do charismatic people do? Well they obviously appeal to our collective aspirations and fantasies, and they are very skilled at creating rapport, using all the behavioural techniques mentioned in previous chapters to strengthen our sense of identification with them. They can identify common understanding and needs, and build these into a collective vision which appeals as much to our imagination as to our reason.

Charismatic people communicate a conviction and purpose which overrides their ego-gratification. They are beyond needing to have their self-confidence constantly reinforced by others. Dr Max Atkinson, who researches how great orators communicate has discovered that one of their techniques is to resume speaking before applause has died down, reinforcing the impression that their message takes precedence over the appreciation they are being shown by the audience.

Dr Atkinson has also discovered that the speeches of great orators are structured upon several simple devices: lists of three, repetition, and comparisons and contrasts, all of which make communication more accessible because they reflect our own thinking processes.

So, it would appear that charisma can be learnt – by anyone who has sufficient self-motivation to apply the many techniques described in these pages.

CONFIDENCE TRICK: Planning for Professionalism

Even when we're quite successful, we need to keep giving ourselves new goals, to keep our levels of motivation high. In summary then, from this chapter, can you give yourself any of the following goals to develop your professionalism:

- Learn new skills and disciplines.

- Network more effectively.

- Use communication more strategically.

- Position yourself for career opportunities and job interviews.

- Get yourself media exposure.

- Improve your performance in meetings and presentations.

- Develop confidence and charisma.

Specifically decide on up to three goals, and plan how and when you will achieve them. Good luck!

14 Passing on Confidence

CONFIDENCE KEY: Helping other people to build their confidence

THE Hawthorne research studies are perhaps the most famous in occupational psychology. Led by Elton Mayo, a Harvard academic, they were designed to establish the relationship between work conditions and the morale of employees at the Hawthorne Plant of the Western Electric Company in Chicago, in the 1920s and 30s. An unexpected by-product of the research was that the morale of the workforce improved considerably. A new phenomenon at work was identified: that people feel much better about what they are doing when others show an interest in them and give them attention. Common sense, you might say, but up until that point, people at work had been regarded as programmable machines, to be controlled, punished and occasionally rewarded.

There is still quite a lot of this destructive attitude around, which doesn't help those on the receiving end to build their confidence. Many of the techniques and skills I've described in this book do, because they apply as much to the development of others as they do to ourselves. And it is a truism that in helping others to grow we also help ourselves. In effect, this last chapter is a summary of many of the main points already made in previous chapters, put into the context of helping other people to gain confidence.

Spreading Confidence

This is a marvellous thing to do. Great leaders and visionaries do it: the Martin Luther Kings of this world. Through giving others confidence, we can show them potential they never thought existed, and help them to live fulfilling lives. We can help them to be proud of their achievements and to achieve even more through accepting challenges. For us too, the rewards are immense. We learn about human nature as we watch others grow. We can see people gaining insight, using their resources, changing and developing before our eyes. And because confidence is in limitless supply, helping them to acquire this asset need never be to our detriment. Here's how to do it:

Give people flexible structure frameworks and options

We have to accept that we live in a very uncertain world – a dynamic, changing one. This creates great opportunity for the flexible and people who have several options to choose from. When we increase our confidence we extend how we think and what we do. We help others gain confidence when we help them to become aware of different options and the steps they need to take to achieve what they want.

Confidence is not about one rigid right way. It is about becoming aware of choices and the frameworks we can use. It is about relishing uncertainty rather than trying, in a futile fashion, to destroy it.

Understand that people interpret the world in a highly subjective manner

When we help others become more confident, we need to realise that they may have fears that are completely outside our range of understanding and experience. What motivates us need not necessarily work for them. We need to get them to talk about what is holding them back and then to gently suggest ways of dealing with this. We also need to establish whether they have a clear idea of what their rewards will be for becoming more confident, because the more motivated and focused they can become, the more likely they are to achieve this aim.

Help them dispute their rogue rules

We can talk about what rules they are giving themselves and whether these rules are always rational and supportive. Helping someone to identify and change a rule like, 'I must always be liked', or 'I must always succeed in every situation', can transform how they see themselves approaching challenges. You'll gather that helping others to become confident is again about developing your own listening skills, so that you can support them by your attentive silence.

Use the idea of role to help them clarify their aims and other people's expectations

Talking to people about the roles they play can help them sort out what they are doing out of duty, and what it is they are confused about in their lives. They may be imagining they have to do things as part of a role – loving daughter, responsible husband – when more direct communication between them and the other parties involved, could establish whether or not this is the case. Very often, it is not.

Encourage people to make choices that suit their individual personality preferences

Making people aware that we have different personality dimensions and preferences as described in the latter part of Chapter Three, can help set goals and take decisions according to who *they* think they are, rather than what other people want them to be.

Suggest to people that they cater for their inner and outer selves

Some people need to rebalance the amount of concern and energy they put into their 'inner' and 'outer' lives. Ignoring the need for spiritual confidence, they may feel lonely and want to believe that confidence is all about outwards show. Highly introspective individuals, on the other hand, may need to realise that being accepted as confident by the world, involves projecting a confident image going at least halfway towards meeting others rather than living in a vacuum and wondering why nothing exciting ever happens.

Involve people in goal-setting

When people are feeling frightened about working on their confidence, they may camouflage this by being tentative and vague. Sit down with them and get them to articulate their specific goals aloud or write them down on paper, and the steps they will take to get there. Bearing in mind that I stressed the importance of regular feedback to make goal-setting effective, set up regular times when you meet to review progress.

Becky Cornfield, who writes books about career development, is a friend of mine and is wonderful at making others become effective. If I tell Becky I want to do something, then she will put a date in her diary for several months later, when she will call me to discuss progress.

Get the timid to learn assertiveness skills

When people have been behaving in a habitual way for years, then they will need plenty of hard work and practice to learn new habits. Understanding that we can say what we want, even though getting it may mean compromise, can be very helpful in confidence building.

Work with them on confronting criticism

This book has been most enjoyable to write. This is largely because the Editorial Director at Piatkus, Gill Cormode, and I know one another quite well, and she is skilled, sensitive but also direct in the way she gives criticism. I have benefited greatly from this very positive, constructive feedback, as has the whole project. Learning to handle criticism constructively so that others will feel comfortable in offering suggestions, is invaluable in building confidence. Awareness of our rogue rules is essential – especially ones like, 'I must never fail.'

Help them to become their own best critics

Opening a sensitive conversation with, 'How did you think that went?' is helpful. Many of us need a great deal of retraining, to get into the: 'This is what I've done well', followed by: 'This is where I could improve', sequence. When morale is low, get the person to talk about the specific skills they used in previous achievements. When they are feeling daunted, encourage them to work on improvements that are quite easy to achieve, and to break their goals into smaller chunks.

Treat the people you are helping to develop as adults

It's very easy when we're helping others to develop to allow them to play the compliant child, while we act as nurturing or sometimes critical parents. While helping others to build their confidence, we will need to play the parent *sometimes*, but our aim should be to develop a relationship in which two adults communicate on a similar level. When we make others too dependent on us, we reduce their power.

Use unconditional positive regard with people you are helping develop

To treat others as though they are intrinsically worthy and deserving of love and respect, is a magnificent way to behave. And it can make up for damaging and destructive pasts. Of course, we may need to make it clear sometimes that the person's behaviour is not deserving of love and respect. It's the difference between: 'John, you're a bad boy', and 'John, throwing your porridge across the room is bad behaviour'.

So that's it – twelve steps to help you in helping others to build their confidence. I hope this book inspires you to do so.

Looking On The Bright Side

We need optimism and enthusiasm in this age of uncertainty. The self-centred years of the 1980s have left many of us disillusioned. We are sensing that perhaps we should become more generous and tolerant in our attitudes: that connecting with other people, and social interest and concern for the community matter more than we thought previously and make our lives more meaningful. Businesses like the Body Shop, and Ben and Jerry's ice-cream in the USA, who champion idealism as part of the core of their business values, though targets of criticism, dare to experiment and blaze a trail. Somehow, we all need to find a balance between individual responsibility and concern for the community. It's my belief that self-help and self-development is all part of this – and can be as much about 'us' as it is about 'me'. We must learn to understand ourselves and others better. I hope this book helps you do that.

Further Reading

Analysing Organisations by Sandra Dawson (Macmillan)

Assertiveness at Work by Ken and Kate Back (McGraw Hill)

Cognitive Therapy and The Emotional Disorders by Aaron Beck (Penguin)

Games People Play by Eric Berne (Penguin)

Human Relationship Skills by Richard Nelson-Jones (Cassell)

I'm OK – You're OK by Thomas Harris (Pan)

Inquiring Man: The Psychology of Personal Constructs by Don and Fransella Bannister (Routledge)

Life And How To Survive It by Robin Skynner and John Cleese (Methuen)

Mindfulness by Ellen J Langer (Harvill)

Our Masters' Voices by Max Atkinson (Methuen)

The Personal Growth Handbook by Liz Hodgkinson (Piatkus)

Personal Power by Philippa Davies (Piatkus)

The Successful Self by Dorothy Rowe (Harper Collins)

Time On Our Side by Dorothy Rowe (Harper Collins)

Type Talk at Work by Otto Kroeger with Janet Theusen (Delta)

Wanting Everything by Dorothy Rowe (Harper Collins)

What is Rational-Emotive Therapy? by Windy Dryden and Jack Gordon (Gale Centre Books)

Your Total Image by Philippa Davies (Piatkus)

Helpful Addresses

Institute of Complementary Medicine, PO Box 194, London SE16 1QZ
Tel. 0171-237 5165

Society of Teachers of the Alexander Technique, 20 London House,
266 Fulham Road, London SW10 9EL   Tel. 0171-351 0828

For details on counselling:

Westminster Pastoral Foundation, 23 Kensington Square, London
W8 5HN
Tel. 0171-937 6956

For guidance on your appearance contact:

Irene Nathan, IPR Group, Mallory House, 27 Verulam Road, St Albans,
Herts AL3 4DG   Tel. 01727 844266

Index

abundance thinking, 74–5
accents (regional), 92–3, 102
accessories, 182, 186
achievement needs, 83–5
affirmations, 73–4
Aldefer, Clayton, 83
Alexander technique, 66, 94, 171
alternative therapies, 64–75
Analysing Organisations (Dawson), 189
appearance, 174–87
　body language, 162–73
　changing self-presentation, 50–1
appraisal, 41
　personal account, 77–8
aromatherapy, 66
assertiveness skills, 115–27
　helping others, 202
　personal account, 56
Atkinson, Dr Max, 197

Bandler, Dr Richard, 129
blaming, 31–3
blushing, 107
body language, 162–73
　clothes/accessories, 174–87
Breathing control, 95–6
bullying tactics, 34–5

charisma, 197
childhood influences (negative):
　exorcising, 30, 72
　personal account, 21
　seeking professional help, 27, 42
　self esteem and, 27
clothes/accessories, 174–87
competence:
　fear of lack of, 36–7
　rogue rules and, 39
compliments, 125–7
confrontation:
　de-personalising, 62
　fear of, 33–4, 87, 156
constructs (priorities), 47–50
　goal setting and, 80
　stress and, 149
control:
　fear of loss of, 35–6, 109–10

　rogue rules and, 39
cosmetics, 186
counselling, 27
criticism:
　giving criticism, 122–3, 202
　over-sensitivity to, 41, 49
　rejecting constructive criticism, 37
　resistance to, 31
　taking criticism, 118–23, 202
　thinking critically, 43
cultural values, 26–7, 38

Dawson, Sandra, 189
decision making, 61–3
dental care, 169, 170–1
disabled persons, 43–4

Edwards, Gill, 73, 75
envy/jealousy issues, 23, 75, 82
extroversion/introversion, 58–9
eye contact, 162–3, 171–3

fears, 33–7
　confronting, 67–8
Ferguson, Andrew, 73
'fight or flight' response, 150, 166

game spotting, 144–7
Games People Play (Berne), 139
genetic influences, 20–1
gesticulations, 167
goal-setting, 76–81
　helping others, 202
　ideal role, 57
Grindler, Dr John, 129

hairstyle, 185–6
Handy, Charles, 190
Hawking, Stephen, 30
Hawthorne research studies, 199
humour, 43

image, 174–87
interviews:
　appraisal, 41, 77–8
　body language and, 162, 165, 172
　negating responsibility, 32–3

About the Author

Philippa Davies runs her own business, Voiceworks, which trains top business executives, TV newsreaders and presenters, and the general public in communication and presentation skills. Her clients include Glaxo, Thomas Cook, Coutts Bank, Marks and Spencer, the National Health Service and the Rover Group. She frequently broadcasts on television and radio and is much in demand as a conference speaker.

Philippa took a degree in speech and drama and has an MSc in occupational psychology. She is the author of *Your Total Image* and *Personal Power* (Piatkus) and lives in London.

Further Information

For details of Philippa Davies' Total Confidence and Successful Speaking Skills courses, in-house training and products, please photostat and complete this form and send or fax to:
VOICEWORKS, 223 HAMLET GARDENS, LONDON W6 0TS.
Phone: 0181-748 8318. Fax: 0181-563 7802.

Name: _____

Address: _____

_____